DIRK
BOGARDE

FROM

PENGUIN BOOKS

PENGUIN BOOKS

Published by the Penguin Group. Penguin Books Ltd, 27 Wrights Lane,
London w8 5tz, England. Penguin Books USA Inc., 375 Hudson Street,
New York, New York 10014, USA. Penguin Books Australia Ltd, Ringwood,
Victoria, Australia. Penguin Books Canada Ltd, 10 Alcorn Avenue, Toronto,
Ontario, Canada m4v 3b2. Penguin Books (NZ) Ltd, 182–190 Wairau Road,
Auckland 10, New Zealand · Penguin Books Ltd, Registered Offices: Har-
mondsworth, Middlesex, England · **This extract has been taken from *A Short
Walk from Harrods* by Dirk Bogarde, published by Penguin Books in 1994.**
This edition published 1995 · Copyright © Motley Films Limited, 1993 · All rights
reserved · Typeset by Datix International Limited, Bungay, Suffolk. Printed in
England by Clays Ltd, St Ives plc · Except in the United States of America, this
book is sold subject to the condition that it shall not, by way of trade or otherwise,
be lent, re-sold, hired out, or otherwise circulated without the publisher's prior
consent in any form of binding or cover other than that in which it is published
and without a similar condition including this condition being imposed on the
subsequent purchaser · 10 9 8 7 6 5 4 3 2 1

My chunk of France lay almost dead-centre of a triangle of villages. Well, one proper village, Saint-Cyprien, up behind my land, Le Pré to the west, and Saint-Sulpice to the east. Le Pré straggled along the main road: a bar, some shops, two garages – an Elf and a Shell – a café with a juke-box, and a modest restaurant which served all right-ish food. Occasionally. Saint-Sulpice was not much more than a cross-roads, a monument to its liberation by the Americans on August the 21st, 1944, a row of ageing mulberry trees, a wide *place* where the annual fair and circus was held and, along the road up towards Saint-Cyprien, the olive mill with its enormous wheel. Above the crossroads, on a modest hillock, stood the church with its Provençal flat roof, surrounded by olive trees and cypresses. There were some scattered houses, a churchyard sliding down the hill, the monuments and marble angels looking like a tilting chess set, and at the bottom of all this, neat and trim, the *bureau de poste*. The *bureau de poste* was to play a vastly important part in my life, although I was unaware of that fact in my early weeks – as unaware as I was that, just up the road beyond it, glittering in chrome and plate glass, the Mini-Market, opened in the week I took up my residency, would almost become my pivot.

The mayor of Saint-Sulpice, Etienne Ranchett, a fierce

1

little man with a face like a loganberry, was rumoured to keep a young (and disagreeable) mistress in a hideous little modern villa on the edge of the village. To make life more tolerable for his wife, and avoid gossip, he permitted the erection of the Mini-Market on the old vegetable garden of the house which belonged to his mother-in-law. His wife, a warm-eyed, splendid figure of a woman, Florette Ranchett, became the owner. It shut her up: she turned a blindish eye to the mistress on her doorstep and threw herself with alacrity into the role of shopkeeper in this unlikely modern box set among the olives and rough-walled vegetable garden of her mother's house.

The trouble was that, even with the imposing awning in brown and orange with *Mini-Market* in gold all along its scalloped edge, the glitter and the hum of the freezer, the sparkle and shine of the brilliantly tiled floor (mashed carrot and spinach), in spite of all these attractions no one very much came into the place. Its very glamour put them off and inhibited them. They much preferred the cold, cruddy, dark little shop which had apparently originally stood in its place, run by Madame Ranchett's mother. It was comforting, it had worn linoleum, I was told, fly papers, good bread, and gave credit. In the new shop a new and alarming machine rolled out your bill, all figures and signs, and at the end, after *Thank You for Shopping Here* (in English) there was a more alarming note which, hastily translated, simply said NO CREDIT.

No good French peasant could put up with that for long. And they didn't. They went elsewhere, even if it meant taking the local bus, and Florette Ranchett sat stoically behind her counter, among mountains of lavatory rolls, kitchen paper and serried rows of Harpic, Tide and Omo, on her own. Sometimes, very occasionally, someone would hurry in for something they had suddenly found themselves to be short of, and tourists parked to buy stuff for picnics to take down to the beaches or up into the hills. Otherwise the tins and bottles gathered dust, the stall of vegetables outside under the awning wilted, and Madame Ranchett read *Nice-Matin* from cover to cover six times a day.

I think that the first thing I ever bought from her was a tin of Kiwi dark brown. Her warmth and gratitude was such that I had the distinct impression that I had, by mistake, bought up her entire stock of champagne. She handed me change from my twenty-franc note and explained that the machine was American and that she really couldn't help what it printed on the receipt. Of course she gave credit! In an agricultural village how could she not? They were not millionaires here, depending on the *rose de mai*, jasmine and olives for a living, and sometimes the corn for feed. She was convinced that with patience she could sit it out and that business would become brisk. After all, they all knew and liked her, the mayor's wife and all. Give them time, she'd say, they are as suspicious as goats, and as silly. She was right of course: in time people did begin to drift back – the added bother of the bus, the extra money for the fare, the red pencil ripped through NO CREDIT (a modest suggestion of mine) made it easier, and pleasanter, to run down the hill, across the road, or walk up from the crossroads to do the shopping.   3

Also she had a varied selection of things. She was brave, wise and very handsome. We got on extremely well together, and as soon as she found out that I was a *propriétaire*, had already applied for my *permit de séjour*, and intended to remain in the area for the rest of my life, we eased into a close and affectionate friendship. She never came to my house, I never went to hers. That is not the way in France – a failing of many English people who are neighbourly, if not nosey, and simply don't understand the laws of French family privacy. It works splendidly if you do: you eat together in restaurants but seldom, if ever, dine or break bread at their table. Sensible and a great saving for the cook.

Stuck on a shelf behind the till, with a strip of Sellotape, there was a battered photograph of Madame Ranchett, hair piled high, arms thrown round a dusty American sergeant, laughing with delight. A really pretty woman, enjoying herself on Liberation Day. It was no wonder that Etienne Ranchett had married her, but extremely odd that she had ever married him. However, power comes with the office of mayor, and perhaps that was in the air then. I never asked. But she did admit, one day when I took a closer look at the photograph, that, frankly, the war hadn't been a problem in the village. Until *we* started mucking about down at La Napoule and sending tanks and planes all over the place. They were very handsome, very correct, kind to the old and especially to children. Madame Ranchett had no complaints about the Germans at all.

The Americans, when they arrived, were *far* worse: drunk, stole the chickens as well as the eggs, behaved incorrectly with the young women and cut down the most fruitful olive branches for tank camouflage. They were glad to be free, because it meant that *all* France would be free, but they were quite glad to see the back of the liberators when they finally left.

'Perhaps', I ventured mildly, 'it was different up north?'

She shrugged, sighed. 'Perhaps. But I was not there. I believe in Paris it was bad. Very bad. No food. Deportation. Down here it was easier. They left us alone. Of course we had the Resistance ... but *they* caused a lot of trouble too, really. If they blew up a bridge, well ... how could the farmer get to his stock ... the sheep and goats, the harvest? And then, and then! They would take hostages, the Germans. If you live with the hornet you don't poke sticks into his nest!'

'Well, anyway. It's finished.'

'Thank God. It was bad in England too? Bombs ... the mayor and I went to England. Once.' She shuddered pityingly. 'Never again.'

'Oh. I'm sorry! Why?'

'Look. The ferry was late. It was dark. No signs to London after Ash-Furd. We got lost in some development called Addy-Coombe, I will always remember the name, no one would help us, they looked at us as if we were mad and went away. It was awful. Awful. Then we saw a sign that said *Hotel* ... no food. We were too late. Too *late* at *nine o'clock*! We had to find a café in the dark and we had some white chicken like rubber, and frozen peas like emeralds. And as hard. It was a disaster. A disaster. We drove back to the 5 ferry the next morning. We had to sleep in a terrible place one of your policemen told us about. Bed and Breakfast. Horrible! But there was a big bed. I cried myself to sleep, the mayor drank half a bottle of Scotch he bought on the ferry. In the morning we came back to France. You understand me? I understand why you came here to live. Intolerable! Intolerable! Those peas. My God! I wouldn't even string them on a nylon thread as a necklace. I'll never forget them. Never.'

On the west end of this enchanted triangle of villages there was a small area called Quartier des Groules. A narrow road wound downhill, lined with stone plaster-faced houses. Each had a mounting-block of solid limestone just outside the front door, making it easy for the occupants to mount their ass or donkey, or horse very often, but making life almost out of the question for motorists. The only reason that I mention this is that I had to go to the Quartier every two weeks to take and collect the laundry, for my laundress (and that was her permanent job) lived in a three-storeyed house right at the end. So the hazardous narrow road, bristling with mounting-blocks which would easily have wrecked a tank, had to be negotiated with extreme prudence.

In the first years the Simca Brake just made it; Forwood's Maserati (a fearful bit of showing-off which he loved keenly) never made the first yard, but, later on, the sturdy Peugeot just, by extremely skilful navigation, managed to get down to Madame Mandelli's pretty little terrace. Every two weeks a vast basket of 'dirty' was hauled out of the car, and an
6   equally vast basket of 'clean and ironed' was taken on.

Madame Mandelli laundered like an angel: sheets were ironed and folded into eighteen-inch squares of pristine, crisp splendour, shirts lay flat, ready for stacking. There was a delicate scent of some kind of soap powder, but mainly they smelled of the clean hillside air in which she dried them. At the back of her house, in an area where there was no sign of a flower, rabbit hutch, chicken coop, where no tree existed, where only the blue nylon ropes and coloured pegs reigned supreme, sheets and shirts and pillowcases flew and flapped like bunting at a regatta. Free to the winds of heaven.

In the first months of my life at Le Pigeonnier (that was the name of my place – I don't think I've mentioned it before), a cherished friend and his wife were determined to be 'the very first guests in your new house'. The appalling fact is that by the time they got to me he was already dying from terminal cancer, and his wife was grey with fatigue and despair, desperate to please him, but terrified.

Nevertheless they came. He was determined – his doctors knew there was no hope: they arrived. But it was folly. Almost as soon as he had staggered off the Train Bleu at Cannes he was only capable of being got into bed. The terrible journey had done for him. So, a doctor: rapidly sought in the telephone book by Forwood, who sensibly picked the one nearest to us.

Dr Poteau was a saint. I suppose that is the cliché word, but it, like all clichés, is true for that is what he was. He sorted things out for Robin, as far as he was able medically, but, and this was the worry, he asked if I was capable of changing a bed *three* times a day? I said that I could, I was pretty good at bed-making, mitring all the corners and so on. But what Poteau actually meant at that time was could I wash the sheets? The patient would need changing twice, if not three times, a day because of raging fever. Pyjamas, everything? Had I the means to accommodate this problem? Of course I hadn't. There was no washing-machine. I could iron teacloths and T-shirts fairly neatly, but that was all. There were absolutely no facilities for a dying man with a pile of sodden sheets.

Dr Poteau gave me *his* laundress, Madame Bruna Mandelli, a gesture of the utmost generosity and goodness: I, the English stranger, was overwhelmed. Madame Mandelli had a washing-machine, could take me on – she 'did' for the doctor, his family (his wife having only one arm she could not manage laundering), the local priest and two exceptionally grand 'old families' in the district – for a short time only. She was quite prepared to deal with two sets, or three, of sheets and pillowcases and Heaven alone knew what other bits and pieces. But, she wanted to make clear, she had her regular clients, a limited amount of time, and when my patient had either died or gone back to England, then she would reluctantly have to close my account. As it happened she never did close it: as with Madame Ranchett and Madame Pasquini at the *bureau de poste* (I'll come to her a bit later), my life was enhanced and made glorious by their kindness and affection. One can't do better in life than that.

Bruna Mandelli was a small, compact woman. Italian, from Cremona, she was a superb cook, an industrious house-

keeper, a doting mother of two (a son of four and daughter of two), a loving wife. Her house (actually I only ever got as far as the parlour-kitchen in all the years) was immaculate, sparkling, crammed with china ornaments, flowers and green plants in pots. It was always pungent with the scents of tomato, oregano, basil and freshly made pasta, which she hung in sheets over a broom handle, supported on the backs of two chairs, with a double page of *Nice-Matin* beneath: if you could read the small print through the pasta then it was acceptable. Not otherwise.

Madame Mandelli's hair was vivid henna-red, her strong arms were freckled as a rainbow trout, and she carried a pair of eyebrows, carefully pencilled in maroon half-circles, exactly one inch above the place where her real eyebrows (which she seemed to lack) should have been. Thus she appeared to be in a condition of permanent surprise.

The first two weeks of Robin's visit passed slowly, but moderately well, considering nurses, and potions, and the excellent Dr Poteau. I stripped the bed two or three times a day (for his fever would not abate), pyjamas were changed constantly, towels slung into heaps, and I carted everything off to Madame Mandelli in the big willow laundry basket. Her terrace, at the far end of the little street, was crammed with pots and old enamel pans rioting with impatiens, geraniums, white daisies and cascading pelargonium. They were sheltered from the blazing sun by an ancient mulberry which stood, a bit lopsidedly, dead centre.

This particular morning there seemed to be no one about. The sun burned down, casting dark shadows, but there was no sound of the singing, which was usual, if monotonous; no odours from the kitchen, as there always were, no cheeping and chittering from the budgerigar's cage which normally hung on a hook by the front door. No cage.

Ominously, I saw the basket of 'clean and ironed' standing deliberately on the terrace beside the closed front door. The little red exercise book, used for the laundry list and the account, lay on the top of the folded sheets. The bamboo-bead curtain hung still. No rasp and clatter in the morning wind. Maybe she had gone to town? Unlikely at this hour. I set down my basket of 'dirty' and called out. No response. I called again, louder. Forwood leant out of his car window curiously. I shrugged, called again: 'Madame?' I had to pay for the 'clean and ironed' and check with her the list of 'dirty'.

I was about to make a final attempt when a shutter above my head opened cautiously, and through a frill of medlar leaves, looking rather like a gargoyle, an anguished head peered down. The face was drained. Tears fell.

'Disaster!' she murmured. '*Oh! Dio! Oh! Dio! Catastrophe!*' And shaking her head she recommenced what she had obviously been doing until my arrival, indulging herself in most unattractive weeping.

I held up a fist full of francs. 'For last week's stuff!'

She wiped her face with both hands. '*Scusa! Scusa! ... Momento ...*' she said and I leant against the mulberry watching a stream of ants swarming up and down its trunk.

The door opened, the bamboo curtain was parted. '*Prego ... enter ...*' She did not look directly at me; by the sag of her shoulders she was resigned and hopeless.

'Oh Madame! Excuse me . . . You have such sadness?'

She sat heavily in a chair by the table, head in hands. '*Ecoute moi . . .*' and she was off.

Well, it really wasn't all that much of a disaster or a catastrophe. All that had happened was that her washing-machine had blown up. It was old, out of date, there were no spares, it was unmendable. That's all. But, of course, for Bruna Mandelli, with her clients and large family, it was disaster enough.

Her face was dragged with grief, her eyes red from weeping, her maroon eyebrows smudged into two livid bruises. So distracted had she been that she had even forgotten to remove her pink plastic rollers. I gave her the money she was owed and said that I would instantly go into town and purchase a new washing-machine, modern, with a full guarantee. She uttered a little scream of horror, covered her mouth with her hands, shook her head frantically. 'No! No! *Quelle horreur! Jamais!* Never, never . . .'

I felt as if I had made a fumbled attempt at rape; then of course I realized that I had desperately insulted her as a woman, as a laundress and a person of deep, intense pride. She hiccupped with anger until I explained in my poor French (you really do need a bit more than menu French for this sort of deal) that it was essential for me to get my laundry done, that I would purchase the machine for us all, and that she would do all my washing and ironing absolutely free until such time as she had paid me back. I thought that that made sense?

Gradually, as she unpinned her rollers, she conceded that

it *might* make sense to her. Without the machine she'd be pretty desperate herself, and gravely out of pocket. I reminded her that the priest would be in despair too. All those vestments and the altar stuff? Finally, with a flicking of nervous looks, a blowing of her nose, wiping her face with hard-worked hands, she told me the name of the best electrics shop in town, and with a helpless shrug of resignation, but a verbal agreement that she would do my laundry free until she was out of my debt, she went into the kitchen area, brought out the budgerigar cage and hung it on its hook outside the front door.

As we drove away I looked back and saw that she was carefully arranging a teacloth over it to shade it from the sun. A sign, I felt certain, of acceptance. Storms in the Mediterranean are quite often short and violent.

Two days later, after a deal of tipping here and there, and an instant cheque, not a credit card (viewed with grave suspicion in town) a perfectly gigantic German creation, blinding in white enamel and chrome, was delivered, and fitted, in Quartier des Groules. It appeared to do just about everything except the ironing and the sewing on of buttons. Otherwise it was a miracle machine.

One morning, the day after Robin and Angela his wife had finally managed to get taken off to the airport, with oxygen cylinders, care and attention in abundance, and were headed for London and the final clinic, I opened the front door on to the terrace to let the desperate dogs out to do their pee (we had overslept from sheer exhaustion). I almost tripped over a package wrapped up in red and gold paper, a hoarded piece of last Christmas apparently, to judge by the gold stars and holly sprigs. Inside, a boxed bottle of Chivas Regal.

There was no message.

Everyone knew it as 'the moon country', and that was long before Neil Armstrong set foot on the thing and proved them right. It was a savage, strange landscape, a desolate limestone plateau one thousand metres up. It looked as if a tremendous wall had been pushed over by a giant and had fallen, quite flat, cracked but unbroken, across the mountain top. It stretched for acres, about a half-hour drive from the house, up a sharply twisting road, which gave some people acute vertigo and others what they called 'water brash', so that they were compelled to stare desperately at the back of the person in front and dared not look out of a window or through the windscreen. Coming down, of course, was worse. Usually eliciting stifled moans, swallowing gulps and pleas for a rest. As I didn't suffer either from vertigo or travel sickness, I was fairly soulless.

In the summer months, from May until the end of September, the house became a cheap *pension*. People I had hardly nodded to in a different life suddenly wrote effulgent letters saying that they'd 'be in your area about then, so could we possibly be simply dreadful and ask you to give us a room/bed/board/meal, whatever?' and it was difficult to refuse. Of course, family and friends were quite different, and hugely welcome. But the others were a bit of a pain, frankly. They 13 also cost a good deal. Although, to be sure, some did bring gifts in kind. Like a cheese, bottles of untried wine, fruits or, worst of all, fresh fish from the market in Nice or Cannes or some other port which, by the time they got it to me, had gone off. And anyway, usually (always in fact) their meals had already been planned and catered for, so there was nothing to be done with the fresh 'gone off' fish but chuck it. However, people *did* try.

And, very often, their company on the terrace in the evenings, with a glass of wine and the drifting scent of good tobacco under the vine, was comforting.

However, it was the usual thing to do to go up to the moon country after lunch. Unless it was absolutely blistering (July and August were hellish), they were stuffed into cars and led up the twisting road in order, I always insisted, to aid their digestion. The fact that many longed to throw up the three-course lunch just consumed was neither here nor there. Anyway, to me. The dogs, Labo and a boxer, Daisy, they too didn't give a fig: their screams and shrieks at the mere mention of the word 'motor car'; the very slightest move towards leash and collar turned them into raging tigers.

So we'd set off. Once on top, in the clear, cool air of the plateau, people began to regain their balance and almost quite liked the whole operation. Apart from the descent, that is. However, in the winter it was all very different. The days were shorter, lunch took a little longer, we left the washing-up and went off in that hour or two left just before the light began to fade and the sky drained of colour and the evening star sprang into the pale, clear, winter emptiness as if a switch had been snapped on, heralding the night.

Then we clambered across the corrugations of the honey-combed limestone, the screes of shale and fallen rocks, the low clumps of thyme, box and juniper hiding in crevasses, and round the rims of little sunken fields which had been, literally, scratched, centuries ago, from pockets in the harsh land, raked and tended, each with a cairn of stones and shards ploughed up from the thin earth.

There were no trees at this height – the wind saw to that – just stunted writhen pines, straining to exist, clinging desperately with exposed roots like aged, knuckled fists clutching the steep sides of the scratchings of fallow soil.

In the early spring, clumps of hellebore hung acid-green bells in clusters along the goat tracks, or a wind-wrenched bramble thrust tiny buds against the aching ice-blue sky. In the little fields, or dells, the new barley and wheat were a green gauze, as thin and sparse as a hair transplant. Crows and ravens stalked about grubbing, or seeking twigs and straw for nests. Sometimes, but very rarely and only when the dogs had capered miles away, you might catch a fleeting sight of a wildcat, but they melted into the thyme and rock-hugging juniper and myrtle. And one was never really quite certain that they had been there, otherwise the silence sang, and only the distant tonkle of a goat bell or the very vaguest whisper of trickling water from a hidden spring broke the perfect glory of the silence.

The summer, of course, was quite another matter. Fat green lizards baked on the oven slabs of limestone, vipers swung and curled away into the cracks and crannies, and in the places where the little springs had made modest pools among the tumbled stones, tadpoles wriggled and dived in the crystal, cold water.

However, in the winter these same springs and pools froze solid, looking shiny, like molten glass spilled across the rocks, dragging ragged curtains of icicles where they had started to trickle over ledges, until the frost had stilled them and frozen movement.

But in early spring, and before the day trippers arrived from the coast, on the high plateau the landscape was benign and sweet. Every patch of grassland was sheeted with great drifts of blue and gold crocuses, white narcissi, cowslips, clover, scarlet anemones and, in the sheltered cracks of the rock, clumps of tiny cyclamen: their combined scent on still days was overpowering, the humming of a trillion bees foraging for nectar filled the air.

Sometimes, driving up from the plain, one could be in for a surprise, although very often I was warned ahead. Washing up at the sink, I could see the top of the mountain from the window plumed with cloud, which meant that the voyage up would be hazardous. Zig-zagging up and turning at one of the steep bends, there would suddenly be a solid wall of dank, dripping, drifting fog. Visibility down to a couple of metres, sidelights on; windscreen-wipers squealed and whispered, moisture dripped and beaded and the rare car coming towards one would inch slowly past in the thick gloom, lights faded to amber through the mist, number-plates almost unreadable. The silence was odd. Profound, empty. One felt absolutely alone, isolated, with no connection to the world so recently left behind on the plain below. And then, very slowly, the fog would rip into shreds; it would tear and rend, whirl and fray, melt into tatters and suddenly, within an instant, it had gone, spiralling aloft into a sky as clear and sparkling as polished glass, blue as cornflowers. No clouds. Glittering, brilliant, washed and sharp-edged.

At the top of the pass a new world lay ahead. Looking back, the great bank of fog loomed sullenly, a sombre blanket of boiling cloud, dark and impenetrable, cold, clinging. It always amazed me that we had driven safely through.

The air up there was cool, the distant hills softer, greener, the far mountains of the pre-Alps jagged against the porcelain blue. At the far edge of the great tumble of limestone rock, proper fields, not the scratched little dells in the stone, were lush with serried rows of potatoes, peas, beans, carrots. People worked among the crops, stooping, striding, stacking boxes brimming with 'early' vegetables for the markets down on the plain, exhausted now by the heat. But, in time, even up there at this height, in June and July, all this bounty was shrivelled by the burning sun. The spring flowers went as swiftly as they had arrived and succumbed to the relentless heat in the high, pure air.

Up there the houses, too, altered. No longer Roman-tiled roofs and vines for shelter, no olives: now sharp-roofed chalets, with wooden balconies and log stacks amidst sentinel firs set among beech and poplar trees. A mountain landscape and a mountain people. Provence was always surprising.

Madame Pasquini was the *chef de bureau* at the post office in Saint-Sulpice. A trim little woman, she managed her *bureau* with enormous efficiency, dealt with stamps, pensions, parcels and the telephone cabinet in the corner of her small room from behind a high counter. One of the pleasantest sounds I could hope to hear was the *Bang! Bang! Bang!* as she franked the day's mail ready to be sacked and collected by the yellow mail van for the sorting office. It meant that I had not actually 'missed the post'.

Her office was sparse: apart from the counter, some scales, a pickle jar of wild flowers and the telephone, there was nothing there to make one linger. A deliberate effect: even her little pot-bellied stove for use in the bitter winter was well behind the counter so no one could huddle round it and have a chat. She was far too brisk and busy for that sort of life. When I first got to the village she was, if anything, distant. I was unfamiliar with the cost of stamps and the various bits and pieces of money. I know I often irritated her, but she did her best to say nothing. And it was only when she discovered that I had obtained my *carte de séjour*, allowing me to stay in the area of the Alpes Maritimes for six months, and after my indication that my stay would be permanent, that she eased up on coolness and allowed herself a flinty smile. That vanished, the flintiness, after an encounter we had up in the moon country. Vanished for ever.

She had a little red Renault and a large, hairy dog. I don't know what sort of dog it was . . . a mix-up, but it was aged and she adored it. She felt secure with it curled up on a strip of grubby carpet at her feet. No one would cosh her or rob the till with Joujou about. The fact that Joujou had a sparse allowance of yellow teeth and rheumy eyes and had to be well into late, if not old, age seemed not to have occurred to her. Or perhaps it had? Anyway, she set it aside, as people do, and refused to consider the facts before her.

Driving through the limestone rocks one Sunday afternoon, I saw the red Renault parked far ahead by a stone basin into which a spring gently bubbled. Up on the top of the ridge, hard against the skyline, a tiny figure windmilled frantic arms.

'I think that is Madame Pasquini, waving away up there,' I said.

'Fool of a woman! Run out of petrol probably. Women. Honestly, hopeless about cars . . .' Forwood was always dismissive of women drivers, but he did, that time at least, start to slow down as the figure up on the ridge came scrambling towards us, arms flailing, legs skittering about on the rock and shale.

She was calling out, but for the moment (windows closed, dogs squealing with excitement, the air conditioning belting – it was the first really hot day of spring) she was soundless. I got out and began to clamber up towards her, waving back, I suppose to reassure her that I was on my way? Idiotic the things one does.

As we came together, she looked wretched, untidy. Hair ragged, stockings torn at the knee, one sleeve up, one down. A lady with a problem: a dead body? A sheep? It was quite obvious that *she* had broken nothing, she was so energetic, but her voice was hoarse with desperation.

'Monsieur! Ah! *Grâce à Dieu! Aidez moi.* Help me! I have a terrible catastrophe! Come quickly, come quickly.' She turned round and scrambled back the way she had come. I was bound to follow. It was a perilous journey skidding about on the rock. There were sudden little pits, crevasses, clutches of juniper and box: a fall, a trip even, would mean a fracture or a break.

At the top, lying in blazing sun beside a clump of thyme, was the inert body of Joujou, eyes already glazing, tongue slightly protruding. Clearly dead. Flies on its muzzle.

Madame Pasquini fell to the rocks on her knees and grabbed a foot. 'Can you help? It was a viper! I saw it . . . lying on the rock . . .'

I squatted beside her, opened one of the dog's rheumy eyes wider than it already was, looked at the tongue, felt, idiotically under all that thick hair, for a heartbeat. 'Madame, I regret he is dead.'

Forwood, breathless and irritated, had caught up with us.

'Madame Pasquini's dog has been bitten by a viper.'

'I see. Is it dead?'

'Very.'

Forwood addressed himself to the weeping *chef de bureau* in French, asked: how long ago? About half an hour. She couldn't do anything to help it. It went into a coma almost instantly, it was old. Then Forwood announced the grim news himself. '*Il est mort, Madame. Hélâs!*'

For a moment she remained on her knees, the sun beating down on the rocks. She ran a hand through the shaggy hair, shrugged gently, rose to her feet. '*Alors . . .*' she said.

20

We carried the dead animal down the hill. It was a hefty weight, and Forwood, I knew, was not absolutely delighted: he'd got on an Italian shirt of which he was particularly fond. However, apart from the droplets of blood on the muzzle, there was no mess, and we dumped the corpse, with its lolling head, into the Renault boot and, with a silent hand-shake all round, watched Madame Pasquini drive away.

Almost from that moment on she and I – well, all three of us really – became very good friends indeed. Nothing was said, there were no particular thanks given: there was merely a flow of pleasant understanding and patience when I bundled about with 'four stamps, airmail for South Africa, ten for Japan, eight normal for Germany, twenty-four for the UK and a fat envelope of manuscript for Hitchin, Herts', where my excellent typist, Sally, was ready to make sense from chaos. This was the usual weekly deal at the *bureau de poste*. Madame Pasquini got very used to the constant fan mail, and the stamp prices and fluctuations, and knew, instantly, that the buff envelope with the manuscript had to be registered, crayon-crossed and labelled '*Exprès*'. '*Tiens!* Another book! Monsieur Dickeens!'

When she went away on her holiday, usually to Brittany, she always sent a card to say that she was having 'pleasing *vacances*, with very good food and just a little wine'. And, one time, shortly after Joujou's death, I bought a small puppy of mixed breed from a gipsy child, who was dragging it about on a rope in the Marché Forville in Cannes, and, cautiously, placed it on Madame's counter beside the jar of lilac and the scales. Her immediate cry of delight, '*Oh!* 21

Comme il est beau! Si *beau!*', and the fact that she took it into her arms right away indicated that, should I suggest she might accept it, she certainly would. And did. And thus was formed a firm bond which was never broken. The creature grew to reasonable size (no giant), was spirited, pleasant, loving and a wild mixture of perhaps a hound and a spaniel – one could never know what breeds had been utilized. And she didn't care anyway, and called it 'Jack' . . . because that was an English name. The logic escaped me, but then most French logic did anyway. However, gradually I was peopling my new life with good friends who would remain with me. And they did.

It was an agreeable sensation for a foreigner in a strange land. A feeling of 'joining', being accepted. More 'belonging'.

One day, checking the list of cleaned and ironed on Madame Mandelli's table in her spotless kitchen, sorting out franc notes for payment, I said something about having to get a wall built at Le Pigeonnier as a shield against the savage mistral which roared straight across the terrace and ripped flowerpots, rakes, brooms and garden chairs across the hill and thrashed the shutters, and made life generally exhausting. I, personally, detest wind: it makes me restless and irritated. It was a phenomenon that no one had bothered to tell me about, this mistral. I mean, I knew it blew, I knew what it *was*; but I had not the very least idea that it came careering down the Rhône valley, which was miles away, turned sharp left when it hit the sea, and raged straight up the valley to blast my house and land, head on, rending the roof tiles into confetti, the trees into tatty feather dusters. Something had to be done pretty quickly about a deflecting wall, a barrier. Bruna Mandelli pursed carmine lips, shook henna-red hair, sighed, and said that she detested the mistral because it made her so *fatiguée*, and that her husband Rémy was a splendid *maçon*, and would I like him to come to the house to talk about the idea? She could, she said, hand on heart, recommend him as the best *maçon* in the district, and probably the best entrepreneur and *maçon* between Ventimiglia and Toulon. And he would be 'fair' and had worked at the house with the previous owners. Indeed, he and she had first met there in the stable (now a part of my Long Room) during the war, when they were very young. He knew every stone and tile. He was a suggestion that I simply should not refuse. I am always extremely grateful to the Fates, and Bruna, that I did not.

Rémy Mandelli was pretty large – six foot something – muscular, handsome, with a cloth cap permanently at the back of his head, a Gitane on his lower lip, a flash of gold when he grinned or laughed. His handshake was strong, his accent thick Provençal (unlike his wife he had been born in the area), and his energy was unlimited. He was to prove an excellent *maçon*, as had been promised, and, in the end, a loyal friend. Perhaps his ideas and mine did not always coincide: he was longing to rip out everything that was old and beautiful and stuff the house with factory tiles, chrome and glittery brass, and was constantly bewildered when I discovered a store of ancient tiles in some abandoned farm building, or a battered oil lamp with a ruby-red glass shade 23 in a *brocante*, and he found it hard to come to terms with my insistence that the plaster in the house should be, at all times, rough-rendered, with the brush marks showing. This threw him into a great fuss. '*Malheur!* People will judge my work is careless! That I am a peasant!'

He was even more bewildered, and irritated, when he was asked to strip down all the beams in sight to the bare, glorious, silvered oak. Coats and coats of brown or yellow paint peeled off like potato skins, and his glum look when I praised his work, his shrug, his disgusted pottle of spit into a discreet corner, forced me time and time again, to comfort him with the firm arm of friendship and a chatter of clucking praise.

In the end, after some two years, he began, very cautiously, to come round to my way of thinking, and eventually it was Monsieur Rémy who crowed with delight when, wrecking some old building across the valley, he would salvage things which he would normally have rejected as 'ancient rubbish' for the treasure which I considered them to be. Eventually, his battered truck would bump up the track bearing an ancient beam, a slithering of floor tiles, stacks of roof tiles, or a plate rack covered in dust and thick cream or brown paint which concealed a solid, carved olive wood glory.

He once brought his parents up to have a look. They would, he assured me, be astonished to see that I had re-created exactly what they had spent their lives, and a great deal of money, getting rid of.

'It's like a museum!' he cried, and the parents, aged, gentle, she all in black, he in the church suit, cap in hand, rosebud in his buttonhole, came to Le Pigeonnier and marvelled silently to see the re-creation of an almost forgotten way of life. I hasten to add that at no time did the house ever qualify for the cover of *House and Garden* or the *Architectural Review*. It was simple and undecorated.

They were bemused, his parents, by the fact that there was no television set, no cocktail cabinet; that there were no curtains, only shutters; and that the huge fireplace burned only logs, that the floors were uneven and polished like glass.

Like my own mother before her, Madame Mandelli senior sighed that there was no carpet, that the lamps were mainly oil, that the beams were stripped and on display and not concealed tidily in the ceiling. Anyway, they were extremely polite, and left with many handshakes and nods of apparent approval. '*C'est comme le temps ancien!*' But the nods, I could see, shortly turned to sad, worried shakes of disbelief as they drove away, sitting in the front cabin of Monsieur Rémy's truck. A mad foreigner! Poor fellow. All that drudgery brought back again!

Of course, Monsieur Rémy and I were not, at any time, the only people at work on the place. Forwood took charge of all the outside work, that is to say the maintenance of the terraces, the pruning of the vines, the spraying, the cutting of the hay, the raking, the never-ending cleaning of the land. This was essential by law, for fear of fire. If the land was not cleaned, the fine was instant and costly. Anyway, one's neighbours in the farms about the area were quick to complain if things seemed lax. Their property was at risk too, and if a fire started in the mistral, everyone was in dire trouble. So the cleaning, or the *débroussaillage*, never ended. Only in January and February was there a little respite; after that everything started to push up again.

I was never any good at machines, certainly not the grass-cutters with which I had to deal: enormous red things with zig-zag blades that belched and roared, had gears and exhausts, and tore away with me. I might just as well have been driving again. It required all one's strength to guide, control and hold them. We had four of these in varying widths. All German. No other country made anything as tough and vicious. They were tanks, frankly. And they did the job. I stayed, as much as possible, around the house and the modest bit of flower garden, which I hacked out of a piece of field, the overgrown *potager*, where I attempted to grow vegetables and herbs, and the pond area. Otherwise I joined Monsieur Rémy and his Troupe.

The Troupe is worth a slight diversion here. It was led by Monsieur Danté, a stooped, grey-haired man of indeterminate age with a drooping moustache, probably no more than fifty. He hardly ever spoke, never smiled, and carried some profound sadness about with him like a pocket watch. From time to time I would see him stop doing whatever he was doing and consider this sadness, shaking his head slowly, sighing, brushing his eyes with an arm; and then, after a blink or two, he'd continue his work. Monsieur Rémy said he'd had 'a bad war', but he was a good worker. Two Arabs made up the rough-work part of the Troupe. One was vaguely retarded, kindly, silent, thin, very strong and an excellent worker with stone. Him I only ever knew as Fraj.

He came from Tunis. The other fellow was very different. About eighteen, medium height, from Sousse, he fancied himself inordinately, glancing from time to time at his reflection in a tiny pocket mirror he carried in his shirt, running a piece of comb through glossy curls, baring his lips in a wide smile to display remarkable, for an Arab, teeth as white as peeled almonds. He was known to us all as Plum-Bum on account of the purple velvet trousers, hacked off at groin level and skin tight, which he wore at all times during work. He had a pretty little wife, of about fourteen or fifteen, who was as often as not, over the years, pregnant and always dragged a small child by one arm behind her like a toy dog on wheels. It usually had a blue plastic dummy shoved into its mouth and a pink and orange knitted cap with a pom-pom on its wobbling head. She never spoke when she sometimes arrived on the site to bring Plum-Bum a message or a packet of food, but would demurely look down, and twist about on her flip-flopped feet with chipped red toenails. They lived together, with about a dozen other Arabs, in an almost derelict building on the edge of the village, and Monsieur Rémy assured me in a hoarse whisper that they were better off than most of their neighbours because Plum-Bum enjoyed unlimited sex with the ones who were without wives. He delighted, said Monsieur Rémy, in 'jig-jig' for money, and never lacked clients. However, he was a good worker, apparently loved his wife and got her pregnant as often as possible. Monsieur Rémy recounted all this with a degree of awe. '*Malheur!*' he would mutter. 'He is a veritable stallion and only eighteen!'

It is highly likely that Fraj, Plum-Bum and his wife were all 'illegals', that is to say Arabs from Tunisia or Algeria who had managed to slip into France via Marseille and melt, tactfully, into the population. They had no papers, but Monsieur Rémy shrugged that off and said that as long as they worked hard, as his two did, got paid in cash, and there was no record, on paper anyway, of them being employed by him, then *tant pis!* He'd pick up another couple if anything went wrong: there were plenty just hanging about waiting to do any kind of work in order to survive. No one could possibly keep a check on them all. Fraj was the only real worry. He could do nothing but build stone walls, at which he was amazingly good, placing stone upon stone with astonishing accuracy. He was kept busy on my terraces for nearly all the time I lived on the hill. It was rather like painting the Forth Bridge, never ending. Sheep skittering across the terraces leapt a wall and brought down a boulder. Fraj patiently rebuilt it, a trace of dribble on his chin, his dull eyes keen for the size and weight of the stone. The only other job he could manage was sweeping up with a long-handled broom. It took him hours.

However, with the Troupe under the eagle eye of Monsieur Rémy, with me offering my untutored assistance, and Forwood on the terraces, we all managed very well. In time the dark pit with the stone sink in a corner was gutted and transformed into a spanking modern kitchen, a garage built against the north wall, a pond dug where the cesspit pipes had cracked and leaked into a green mossy bog, and the mistral finally deflected, anyway from the front terrace, by a stone and beamed *porte d'entrée* hung with a big oak door salvaged from the original kitchen.

The house, as far as I could see, was secured. All that was needed were some trees. Although I had an hectare of ancient oak wood climbing up the hill at the back, there were no trees round the house itself, save for two old pollarded limes planted to shade the terrace. What I wanted was a frame of cypress trees. I didn't want to wait for them. I wanted instant timelessness.

I got it. The trees were carted up from a nursery in the valley, thirty to forty years old, secure in enormous wooden tubs or, rather, *bacs*. These were then inched towards the pits, dug by Fraj and Plum-Bum and lined deep with manure and heavy gravel. The staves of the *bacs* were eased apart and the trees manually slid into place. I bought three originally. Monsieur Rémy insisted that three was the correct number for a Provençal house. Faith, Hope and Charity – or, if I preferred it, the Holy Trinity. Anyway, they guaranteed luck, health and prosperity, and, as he was quick to point out, with no damp-course, the walls built on living rock, the roof riddled with beetle, and the tiles unfixed, at least I would need the luck.

In time, more cypress trees were planted: a grove of five down the slope of the track, one outside the kitchen window, one at the edge of the pond, so that it was reflected in the still water to remind me of the peace and elegance of Hadrian's Villa outside Rome. All nonsense, of course, and vastly expensive.

In order to achieve all this bounty I had to go off and work 29

again. Two depressingly awful films earned me enough for
the kitchen, the pond, the trees and a new electric light
system. The *poteau* had at last been stuck down on the
boundary between Madame de Beauvallon's land and mine,
but the EDF (Electricité de France) agreed to paint it green
to match the olives and it really hardly showed. But we were
at least now connected for the first time to the mains. So I
bought a refrigerator too ... And, apart from breaking my
self-imposed rule of 'no more movies', no great harm was
done. No one ever saw, or remembered, them. I don't think
they even made it on to video.

Florette Ranchett pushed a copy of *Nice-Matin* towards me:
'You see? Soon I will be behind bars. Like a beast of prey.
Ouf! What has happened to the world?' A black, banner
headline: 'ATTAQUE BRUTALE!' Two youths, masked and on
a moped, had stabbed, bashed on the head, and then robbed
the postmistress over at Saint-Matthieu, not far away. She
was near to death in hospital, the youths had escaped, the
countryside was in shock. Naturally enough. If the *bureau de
poste* in a tiny hamlet could be attacked, what hope was there
for the rest of the area? The age of innocence had finally
ended in violence. Within a few weeks (after the unhappy
death of the Saint-Matthieu postmistress) every small village
shop, every post office, had iron grilles slung along their
counters. The simple, easy, trusting village life had finally
finished.

Florette Ranchett said sadly, 'Innocence and kindness have
30 gone. This was a village which the world forgot. We were

bypassed completely! They nearly forgot to liberate us in 1944 because they were up on the main road and we were down here. And now; after all that, the Germans, the Italians, the Resistance . . . after all *that*, our own begin to destroy us! I know what it is, of course . . .' She got up and went to get an ice-cream for herself, from the freezer. 'It's the fault of television. The kids see all this terrible American stuff. They copy, we have not enough police, *et voilà!* It is the end of familiarity, of friendliness, of trust. You'll see!'

Of course I did. Madame Pasquini down at the post office was equally sad, but, at the same time, resigned. Jack could bark but Jack didn't bite. No longer was it possible to lounge against the counter and chat away about the vines, the snow, the heat or the cold, or just about the cost of seed potatoes. Ordinary politeness remained, of course, but village trust faded. No one was ever encouraged to linger by Madame Pasquini, but she had become very much a friend since Jack and was vastly curious about the letters and packets that kept on coming to my address, even though I had made a valiant effort never to reveal my exact location to anyone apart from family and important business links. I suppose it is fair to say that I was her best client. I was in her *bureau* almost daily and spent a modest fortune. Naturally that was appreciated also.

Across the road, facing the post office, set in an immaculate vegetable garden, stood a hideous little modern villa, Les Sylphides, shaded by a great fig tree. Its owner was a retired postmaster. I never spoke to him. He was always, summer and winter, occupied in his garden. Every year the walls of the villa were a smother of morning glories, his roses were 31 bigger than cabbages, his onions ranged in rows as precise and elegant as the dancers whose ballet had given his house its name. His wife, a tiny creature, with neat little feet, cropped white hair, huge round wire-glasses, wrapped about in a spotless floral pinny, was known to me at least, as Madame Moineau. For a sparrow, plucked, was exactly what she resembled. And she twittered and cheeped, tucked into a corner of the counter at the *bureau de poste*. She and Madame Pasquini were inseparable friends. They both, I was to learn, had a burning passion for the tarot cards. Madame Moineau was the absolute queen of the pack, and people from all about came to consult her, from as far away as Cannes, Nice or even Avignon. She was famous for her readings.

However, she had not foreseen the disaster about to befall her way of life in the post office. Now she was on the outside of a great iron grille and poor Madame Pasquini (plus Jack) was locked away behind. Lounging on the counter, idly talking away about the harvest, the price of knitting wool at Monoprix, the dark rumour that a Dutchman had been asking about the empty farm up at Le Foux, all this comforting chitter chatter was now somehow inhibited. If you had a packet to mail it had to go on a revolving plate which took it into the secure part of the office. No longer could you weigh your own goods on the brass scales, stamp the thing, and hand it over to the expert hands of the postmistress. The intimacy had vanished. Madame Moineau still hunched herself into her corner, she was still constantly a presence, but somehow it was not quite the same any longer.

To speak to Madame Pasquini she felt forced now to raise
her voice, and this grievously embarrassed her. So she sighed,

nodded about at whoever was present, and curtailed her conversations. Her tarot cards had not revealed, either, the enormity of the *real* disaster which lay ahead in her gentle, fragile path.

One day she was not in her corner . . . the next day . . . and the next. I asked if she was perhaps indisposed? On holiday? Madame Pasquini, certain that no one could overhear us (there was only one noisy English tourist in the telephone cabin trying to get a call through to Flaxman. I heard him spelling it out alphabetically in desperation: 'F for . . . *France*, um . . . L for *Londres*, A for, umm . . . *Au revoir* . . .'), said, 'M'sieur is ill. Very ill. They don't know what is wrong. Perhaps a *thrombose*.' This continued for a week and then one day he was whipped off to hospital.

Madame Moineau spent all her days there, tending her beloved man. The garden slowly became neglected, the dead blooms hung on the morning glory like dirty handkerchiefs, weeds sprang up among the onion rows, the roses budded, opened, were spent and fell, the shutters remained closed.

'Why is she always at the hospital? Does she stay there?'

'Until the evening. Then she comes here to sleep. She has to help the nurses.'

'I don't understand? Doesn't she get in the way?'

'He wants her there. He is very alarmed. She takes her crochet. It comforts him. It is his first time in hospital.'

'Is it grave?'

She shrugged, stamped a pile of tourists' postcards, a job she detested. *Bang! Bang! Bang!* 'I think perhaps it is. They do not say. She helps to change his sheets and so on . . .'

33

'Change his sheets? Can't the nurses do that? She is so tiny . . .'

Madame Pasquini gathered the cards into a bundle and bunged them into the thick sack ready for the evening collection at five-thirty. 'How can the nurses change his sheets if he is in the bed? Madame gets him out, he trusts her, and sits him on a chair while they do their work.'

'I see . . .' I didn't, of course. French logic. How can they make your bed if you are lying in it? Worrying. But I asked no more, and during the next few days we did not speak about the owner of Villa Les Sylphides, until one afternoon I heard dreadful, wrenching cries coming through the open window of the *bureau*. Madame Moineau was clasped tightly in Madame Pasquini's arms. She was destroyed with sobbing and every now and again uttered terrible howls of grief. I was about to quietly leave but Madame Pasquini called me to please stay. She would take Madame across to the villa. Perhaps I would telephone Madame Ranchett to come quickly to Les Sylphides – the number was on the wall? . . . And mind Jack?

I was left alone in the post office. I could have robbed the till. Anything. But I called the Mini-Market; Florette Ranchett said she would come down right away, was it *grave*? I said yes. *And* serious. There is a distinction in France.

Fortunately for me, no one came in, no one asked for a stamp, no one wanted to use the telephone or demand their pension. I just sat on a stool beside the dog until, in a few moments, looking pale and naturally distressed, she returned briskly, shut herself firmly behind her cage. She thanked me and said that Madame Ranchett was now in charge, the doctor was on his way with a sedative. Fortunately they had found a bottle of cognac to calm her down. Later on, she said, she would go across and stay overnight in the villa. 'Jack will keep me company. *Hein?* Jack? Guard Maman?'

I asked for the stamps I needed. She tore them out from the stamp-book, pushed them under the grille, did a little sum on a piece of paper. Back to business.

'Twenty-five francs.'

I gave her the money. 'Can I ask you what has happened? Can you say?'

She looked at me sharply, her eyes were red. '*Si. Si.* I can say. It is catastrophic. Catastrophic! Sweet Saviour, give us help . . .' She shut her eyes tight.

'His heart? Has something happened because of that? Thrombosis they said?'

'I told you that. Yes. But it is not so. He is not dead . . . better that he were . . .'

'Not his heart?'

Suddenly she came from behind her counter and cage, crossed the tiled floor, slammed the front door, turned the key, and leaning against it, head down, she said: 'They have cut off his legs. Both his legs!'

'Oh God! But why . . .'

'An error! There was *nothing wrong* with his legs! An error . . .'

'*An error!*'

'They didn't know who he was. The papers were mixed up. They thought he was someone else. There was nothing wrong with his legs!'

She unlocked the door, went back to her counter. '*Voilà!*' she said, now composed.

In a daze of dismay I began to stick stamps on my envelopes.

'You recall? His garden?' she said suddenly. 'He worked in his garden every day, winter and summer. Nothing wrong with his legs. Nothing! An error!' She was collecting my letters in a pile, picking up her franking seal.

Out in the car park I looked across to Villa Les Sylphides. The shuttered windows, the ragged garden, a teacloth and an apron twisting listlessly in the soft wind. From behind me, through the open window, Madame Pasquini was preparing for the evening collection.

Bang! Bang! Bang!

I remember the moment that I first saw the house. I remember the date, even the precise hour. We drove up into Saint-Cyprien for the first time on a crisp, gusting morning. The trees were turning, leaves spinning up and off into tossing thickets. The sun was high, the sky that intense Ricketts blue of childhood: brilliant, hard, washed clean by the recent mistral, it sparkled like a polished mirror. In the square outside the *mairie*, a tricolour snapped and pulled at its white pole, people clustered round the war memorial; collars up against the wind, hands thrust into pockets, they were joined by a wavering procession from the church. I saw the wreath of blue cornflowers (for the French it is the *bluet*, for us the poppy) for remembrance. Close companions. Round the base of the heroic bronze soldier, the glinting medals on the best suits of elderly men shuffling along behind the priests, sombre in wind-whipped lace and billowing vestments. It was November the 11th.

Unlike the British, the French hold the eleventh hour of the eleventh day of the eleventh month as sacred. A day for remembrance. We just shove everything together on the first convenient Sunday of the month and have an official procession in Whitehall. The personal, family, village and small-town feeling of loss, intimacy and continuity has long been lost to us. Not so in France.

We eased slowly through the procession, running dogs, laughing children, choir boys clattering. The church clock began to strike the hour. We stopped. Moments later, the tinny sound still held, wandering on the air from the final stroke. We sat silent. Then Claire, the agent who was taking us around to view properties, moved on again down a steep lane, slowed her car to inching-pace, and stabbing her finger to the left indicated the next location was below. Through a wood of ancient oaks (with trunks too wide for two men to embrace) hung on the side of a steep rock-faced cliff, I saw, far below, the rippled red-tiled roof of a modest, compact farmhouse, standing four-square to the winds on a green plateau below which spilled terrace upon terrace of great olive trees. Beyond the terraces a little pointed hill crowned by a chapel. Beyond that, a valley. Beyond the valley, golden with fading vines, the jagged line of the Estoril mountains, lilac against the harsh, scoured blue of the sky, and, to the far left, distant, sparkling, dancing in the light, teased by the wind, the mistral-whipped sea, creamed with little flickering waves. I knew then, following behind Claire down the hill, that I must have it. And by the end of December, after many battles, fears, panics and terrors, I got it.

Driving back to Saint-Paul that morning, unwilling to view any other house, I found Simone Signoret at her accustomed place behind the olive wood table in the bar of La Colombe, playing Scrabble. She looked up squinting through cigarette smoke, a Bloody Mary in one hand, a scatter of letters in the other. '*Et alors?* Any luck?' I sat on the end of her bench while she placed her letters on the board carefully. '*U, et E, et T. Voilà! "Taquet".* A word. I win.' She put the cigarette in an ash tray.

'I've found a house. *The* house.'

She nodded slowly, took a sip of her drink, put the cigarette back between her red lips. 'With land? How much land?'

'Twelve to fourteen hectares. Four hundred olive trees, an oak wood. A well. Isolated.'

'Price?'

'About 75,000.'

Her eyebrows rose an inch. '*Francs?*'

'No. No. Pounds. About.'

'Make an offer. It is agricultural, eh?'

'Agricultural. Yes. In poor condition.'

'An offer. It's been a bad year. Remember the *événements* in May? That has frightened a lot of the locals. Another revolution. Make an offer: they're probably desperate to sell.'

Three days later I took her to have a look at the place. From the outside only. The owner was selling without having informed his wife and family, and until I had made a definite offer I was not allowed to return to the area. We had been round once: not enough time really to be certain, unless you were as mad as I.

Simone came up the track from the bottom road, and also had a look through the oak trees on the top road, and declared that it was '*une* vraie *maison*' and that I should make an offer immediately. There were another twelve hectares adjoining, with a crumbling little house, which I could have for a further eighteen thousand quid and a year's option to buy.

I went up to the bar, ordered a beer from Pierrot. He opened it and poured it, watching me thoughtfully. 'You have found a house? Perhaps it's good luck today?'

I said that I had found the house I wanted. Told him where. He grinned and wiped the counter down with a sponge. There was a dull flash of silver, or maybe even pewter, from his rather thin mouth.

'Ah ha! So maybe you will soon be *Monsieur le Propriétaire*? It is possible?'

I said it was possible: I had to make the offer.

'And *then* you give me a little piece of paper. I will ask Maman if it's good for you. It is useful to know and she is never wrong, not once. She was sure about Madame Julia and meningitis, sure about the sheep Monsieur Isoardi lost, sure about the American boy, you remember? Last summer. Dead in the Vallon Rouge and no one knew where, apart from Maman! You give me your paper. I'll find out for you. *Compliments! Compliments!*'

Pierrot, who was somewhere in his early fifties, thin, stocky, balding, gaunt, kind, an excellent barman, heavy handed with the rich tourists, considerate with 'regulars', had an aged mother (with whom he still lived) who was famous in the village, and indeed the whole district, for her predictions. You might have called her a witch, something like that. But she did have an amazing success with her powers, and even the local police, one was assured quietly, had often asked for her help. All you were required to do was write something on a piece of paper, anything at all – a telephone number, a name, a line of a song – and she would hold it in her hand and consider whatever it was you were demanding. And, eerily, she was as often as not correct. So, anyway, I wrote something on a piece of paper and handed it to Pierrot.

I was not superstitious, you understand, merely cautious. But, in any case, after a long session with Forwood, and a longer one with Simone in the evening after dinner, and with a good amount of Estandon Blanc going round the table, I went off to Claire the next morning and made my offer. I did not quibble, agreed what was asked, even though Pierrot and Simone and Madame Titin, who ran La Colombe, looked shocked that I did not bargain, and was accepted.

When I returned from my mission, dizzy with delight, amazed at my audacity, overcome to think that I was in train to be the owner of a chunk of this glorious land, Pierrot poured me a drink and said, in a low voice, that his Maman considered the deal to be very advisable. I'd live in the house longer than she would live. Daunting, but in some way satisfying. As it happened, she was right. And Pierrot was to die before I had to leave. I often wonder if she ever knew *that*. Probably not. And just as well perhaps.

However, I was really quite relieved, after I had made my offer, to know that Maman's prognosis, or whatever you care to call it, was favourable. I would always have had a slightly uneasy feeling if her silver-fanged son had looked solemn and hissed mournfully that the signs were occluded in his usual, uncomfortable, manner of relaying unfavourable information. Although technically the house was mine, the deal having been signed, witnessed and sealed with a glass of red wine, I was, for various odd reasons, unable to take possession of my property until the following April.

However, I did manage to get into the house once or twice with my good architect Leon, who was straining at the leash to rip down walls, doors, and tear up cracked tiles and broken bricks. But that had to wait; all we could do at that stage was plan and arrange and measure. And wander about the neglected land with a suddenly doubting Simone. She was all in favour of the place, but could not really come to terms with the fact that I had voluntarily left my own country to come and live in France and, after years in the business of theatre and cinema, could give it all up and turn instead into a peasant. And, what really worried her, good Communist that she was, a very *poor* peasant. After all the years of plenty, as she imagined, would I be able to adjust to a life on the inhospitable limestone and shale of Provence? Would I really relish the splitting of logs, the mowing of the terraces, the pruning of the trees, the digging and sowing, the rough and tumble of true country life? Without very much knowledge of the French language, without newspapers, without even, at the time, a working telephone? I reckoned that I'd manage a great deal better than she and her husband, Montand, would. *They* would have been wildly out of place on my smallholding. I fitted far better.

But she loved the possibilities of the house, the plans and ideas that Forwood and I and Leon had in mind. I think too that she enjoyed our courage, as she called it, and eventually set aside her very real doubts and joined in with us joyfully.

One evening, driving her back to La Colombe, where she lived when she was not working, in preference to Paris, we stopped at her favourite bar in the square, under a great tree, at Vence. During the early days of the German Occupation she and her mother had kept discreetly out of sight here. Being half Jewish she knew it was prudent to fade into the backcloth of life. The hotel-bar gave them a small room. She worked the tables and washed dishes and glasses and survived.

We sat out on the terrace and ordered a Ricard each; they arrived with a jug of water and just one little flask of water which the elderly waiter set before her.

'*Voilà!* Madame Montand,' he said, 'do you recall these little things? They are nearly all broken now. You served enough of them in your time!' – a small flask, holding just enough water for one measure of pastis, a laughing, winking waiter engraved on its side. She gave it to me. To remind me of the evening and her first visit to the house proper, but also as the first gift for the house. A welcoming present. I have no need to be reminded of that signal event. The flask is still with me, a faded moss-rose stuck in its throat. The two of us are the only survivors of that April evening on the bar terrace in Vence. Seeing it gives me infinite comfort.

When I said that memory comes to me, now, in snatches, it is depressingly true. I chucked all my diaries and papers some time ago, so there is no possibility of being able to sit down and, say, open a diary of 1972 and look up the first Sunday in March or July, or whenever. There is no jerk, no jog, of remembrance there. I can't refer back to anything. So I suppose it is rather foolish to try and fill a book with memories brought back by small things like Simone's pastis flask, or a snatch of song, a drifting scent, a forgotten envelope with half-forgotten handwriting.

However, I do remember many, many things – vividly. I am just not always quite certain of exactly when they occurred. I don't really think it matters much? As long as one remembers a moment, a face, a situation, a planting of trees, a thread of music, the fabric of one's life is still intact, even though the pattern or the dyes are faded. But odd *things* trigger memory. A plastic bag, just now, swinging on the handle behind the door in this small London kitchen. I don't know what is in it, truthfully, it's just a plastic bag with modest bulges; probably the pickling onions. But instantly I am off down the path to Madame Meil with the goat-bag, another plastic bag which always hung on the handle of the kitchen door in a different house, a different country. But I remember it with pin-point clarity. I should, after all, because it was my usual chore almost every evening after having fed the dogs. For some reason, which I now no longer recall, the dogs got fed at five o'clock in the afternoon, not earlier. Perhaps a vet gave that advice? Perhaps it was simply because of the time I gave shelter to the ruin of an abandoned puppy, starving, with shattered leg, ribs like barrel hoops, festooned with worms (literally) and bemedalled with pussy sores. In my kitchen outside Rome one late afternoon, about five o'clock, I, most unwisely as it turned out, gave in to animal supplication and fed him. I say unwisely merely because from that instant on Labo remained. And stayed beside me for fourteen years. It was a brutal struggle between us for survival at first. However, that was dogs' feeding-hour, and it remained so from then on. While they snuffled bowls round the kennels, I took a plastic bag stuffed with all the edible kitchen refuse: green stuff, cold spaghetti, stale bread, plate scrapings, gone-bad peaches, bruised apples, fish heads – whatever a goat would eat a goat got. And as far as I was aware, the only things that a goat did not eat were barbed wire, broken glass or ten-inch nails. Everything else went down easily.

Anyway, that's what Madame Meil always said. She and her husband, Emile, lived in a farm down the lane from me on the de Beauvallon border. It had been an attractive-looking little place: outhouses, haystacks, tin baths hanging, a huge cart, a rusty tractor, scabby mongrel dogs yapping – all clustered round the main house, unremarkable but shaded by two gigantic olive trees, five or six hundred years old, which towered over the whole collection from their position on a high bank on the road just above. You really couldn't see very much for the deep silver-green leaves and the gnarled branches. A flash of tile, a pink wall, the privy roof cushioned with house-leeks, the kennel, a pitchfork thrust into a straw stack. Fragments . . . rather like my memories.

The Meils farmed diligently. She had her chickens and ducks, he his goats: a splendid herd of sable-brown beasts with black faces and hoofs. Very handsome. I don't remember what they were called, but they were rare, valuable, and produced an abundance of milk for the cheeses which Madame Meil made and sold in the village on Saturdays. I was not tremendously impressed by her mahogany brown hard-worked hands. The fingernails hooped in mourning, knuckles calloused, unwashed always. It was extremely difficult to avoid the offered cheese when I took down the goat-bag. I liked goat cheese – liked it greatly. I was just a bit anxious about the proximity of the privy to the shed where the cheese was made. There was the most amazing hum of insect life emanating from that privy. The door fitted well, but had a heart cut into the front at eye level. So that, I assumed, if one was occupied, one still could see anyone approaching. Quite often as I hung the bag on a small spiky branch of one of the olive trees, I would be caught by Madame emerging from the humming privy, tucking in her pinafore, and pulling up her thick grey stockings. '*Ah! Voilà! Monsieur Fauchon! Ah, bon . . .*'

Fauchon is the most famous grocer in Paris, perhaps in the world, and supplies delicacies of all kinds to the rich. I was, of course, Monsieur Fauchon because I brought delicious things down to the goats: the spaghetti, bread, stale cake and so on. It was *then* that I *had* to avoid the gift of a cheese offered in hard-worked hands straight from the privy. It was ungallant of me, I know, but as Forwood always pointed out, tetanus or typhoid can kill, dysentery and meningitis aren't a whole lot of fun either, and so it was wiser to invent any lie rather than accept a gift so primed with lingering, awful death.

'But no cheese? Ah, *dommage* . . . You should have a hat!' she said. Her silver teeth catching the sun, she brushed her greyish hair from a nut-brown forehead. Green-bellied flies hummed and droned round the scaling pine door with the cut-out heart behind her.

'I know, Madame . . . I was in a hurry.'

'But in this sun, *patron*! It's strong at this time of afternoon. Five hundred metres up, we are here. Eh? Dangerous. A hat will keep your head cool and you would also be able to shade your eyes.'

I started up her dusty garden path, past a foam of cosmos, a tumble of Bourbon roses. Apart from goats, chickens and the ducks, Madame gardened wildly, and everything she stuck in flourished; she just literally pushed things in anywhere and they were instantly ablaze with bloom. Very frustrating. I never had much success with such nonchalance and trust. The little garden she had dug out of her farmyard was as vulgar, gaudy and as unlikely as a Helen Allingham print.

'Your roses this year! Madame! Fantastic . . .'

'The goats eat them. Goats are idiots. My man has just put up an electric fence on the lower pasture. You didn't see him?'

I assured her that I had not, but I had seen the goats, huddled together in a far corner of the field. She looked a little concerned, wiped her nose with the back of her hand.

'You did not see my man? Doing the fence?'

'No. Just the goats. In the corner. Watching me. There was a sticker with a little yellow triangle, with a red zig-zag on it.'

She nodded happily. '*Ah! Bon! Exact*. He has done it. That is to show the fence is now electric! To keep the goats from my roscs and from wandering into the road. Madame de Beauvallon drives like a maniac. If you are worried about my goats and the cheese I make, ask Dr Santori . . . he is the vet from town. He inoculates my goats. He knows them well, they are a pedigree herd. You mustn't be afraid of tuberculosis! No one gets it now, from goat cheese. You should speak with Dr Santori. You have your dogs, and one day soon you will have sheep' – a decision not a suggestion – 'Your land *always* carried sheep. Three hundred. You have to have sheep to keep the land clean, in case of fire.'

I turned again by the pink and white cosmos to try and get on home. 'I have two dogs, Madame, therefore sheep are out of the question.'

She came after me, tying the strings of her black pinafore round her waist. 'Why? Two dogs? So?'

'Ticks,' I said.

'*Ah, si*. Now Monsieur Labiche is a good friend of ours.

He needs the grazing; he has a strong flock, three hundred head and some goats. I'll tell him that you don't need your grazing because you have dogs and because of ticks. He will be happy to oblige you, to save you the trouble of mowing and cleaning your land . . . and he needs the grazing so badly. He is a good man, from Feyance . . . I will have a word with my man when he comes in. Labiche is a good man, it is a fine herd. He will be very happy: and so will we. The risk of fire will be less if your land is grazed clean.'

'*Ticks*, Madame. Three hundred head of sheep and some goats! How many ticks?'

'Ah! You must lock your dogs up in a kennel while the sheep are here. We can arrange the time exactly when he brings them to you.' French logic.

'I don't want them! We are cleaning the land very well with our German machines.'

She looked sad. She murmured something about Labiche and how honest he was and he would pay a reasonable amount, but I just went on up the path and closed myself out of her little garden. I waved.

Then, 'Honey!' she called. 'I have good, pure honey. It is from the broom and acacias! It is better for you than sugar. Take it in your coffee . . . for cooking . . . Tomorrow, when you come with the bag, I will give you a comb. My man has it every winter, with lemon, in hot water. He never has *la grippe*. Never.'

I called my thanks and picked my way – I was barefoot often in the summer – across the lane and up into my land,

turned, waved a farewell.

'Your garden is very pretty from here,' I called. 'The olives are beautiful, they are laden . . .'

'*Ah, si* . . . but tomorrow they go. Commençon is coming from Nice to take the wood.' She stood shading her eyes from the westering sun.

I stood frozen. To take the wood? 'Why will they do that? *Take* the trees?'

'My man has sold them. For the wood. Tomorrow you will hear the saws. It will be a lot of work but a lot of money . . .' She moved away, flapping at the dogs, calling, '*A demain!*'

And the next morning the roar and whine of the saws filled the valley and the two giant trees which had overshadowed her house for centuries were brutally felled. For the wood. Probably to make disgusting little pepper mills, bread boards, or mustard spoons and salad bowls. For tourists. Hundreds of years were destroyed in moments. For peasant gain.

The valley never looked quite the same again. And when I went down with the bag the next evening I walked, barefoot, through deep drifts of fragrant, moist, pink sawdust, past the two agonized stumps sticking out of the high bank. Country life.

However much one may desire to be quite self-sufficient, it really is not possible if you are running a smallholding, abandoned for years, and especially if you are a learner, which I most certainly was. By the time the terraces were cut, raked and stacked, the trees pruned (four hundred took rather a long time, and it is a specialist's job – which set me back financially at £10 a tree), logs split, dogs fed, fires laid, brambles hacked, invasive bamboo uprooted, a pond excavated and clay dug for 'puddling', there was not much time left for cooking. One had to eat.

Forwood was good at cauliflower cheese and scrambled eggs. And that was his limit. I couldn't boil water but did manage to cut up kilos of cow's cheek to feed the dogs. This was easy. Mix with biscuits and a bit of boiled cauliflower stalk and they were contented. Which was more than I was after about six months of cauliflower cheese with an apple now and again. This was not thrift, you must know, exhaustion merely: there simply wasn't enough energy left to deal with cooking. Help was essential, and was sought from Florette Ranchett, who as usual knew just 'the couple you seek. Charming, in service for years, *select* and very discreet. They worked for the King of Sweden for many years, and latterly for Lady Brancraig down on Cap Ferrat.'

'They are people you know, Madame Ranchett?'

'No. *Pas du tout*. They were in here yesterday, asking for directions to a house beyond Le Foux . . . they were being interviewed for a situation.'

'But . . .?'

'Ah. The people are Belgian! *Quite* impossible! They are almost as bad as the Arabs. They are frugal and mean. It was unsuitable for them. I told them. I *know* the family at that house.' She shuddered. 'They owe me three months' money . . . Why do I give credit! Why! For the village, of course. For rich Belgians, madness . . .'

Henri and Marie arrived for an interview with me three days later and stayed for five years. After which they retired but were still available to 'house-sit' in an emergency.

They were, it must be confessed, a great deal older than they had claimed to be. Marie must have been in her early seventies but hacked off ten years, and wore a geranium-red lipstick and thick white powder to hide her wrinkles, making her look rather like a dried fig. Henri was probably older, and had dyed his hair a sort of sherbet yellow. I suppose, at one time, it had been fair.

However, they were clearly all that Madame Ranchett had said, and we all liked each other right away. Marie cooked extremely well but would do nothing else, except buttons and darning. Henri, on the other hand, was the house-man and would drive the car to get the marketing, and polish the floors and make the beds. Except that after a short, agonizing trial run with Forwood in the Simca Brake he was never allowed near any machine again unless it was connected to a plug. Like the floor-polisher. He was quite incapable of driving anything. Except a hard bargain when it came to his 'leave' every year.

But we all managed very well, and when, eventually, the time came for them to retire to their small flat down below in the valley, I went to Madame Ranchett again and sought her help. The only problem, and it honestly was not a real problem, was that with Henri and Marie we lost any chance of guest accommodation. Which didn't matter right at the start, but got a bit irritating as the years went on, and we had to farm chums out in the village in one of the not very attractive little hotels.

So this time it was decided that a daily lady was all we needed. Two hours a day, and we would cope with the rest.

Well, we got her. She was discovered by Florette Ranchett wandering round the shop one day, a small child on one hip, looking bewildered. She was Spanish, could speak scraps of French, but with signs and a certain amount of shrieking at each other it was established that she had just moved into the area (a small, neglected house by a junk yard) with a husband who had got a job at the local golf course, mowing the greens. She had no money, or very little, and that day wanted some broken biscuits or stale bread. She could, and did, pay for some milk.

Madame Ranchett called me to alert me and a few days later Soleidad arrived up the track on a sputtering Mobylette, with her awful child strapped into a chair on the back, head lolling, dummy sprouting from dribbly lips. She came round the house with me doing a full tour. I showed her the fridge, the sink, the baths, the beds, the linen cupboard, the china and all the rest. She was silent, feeling a piece of linen between thumb and forefinger here, weighing a glass there, studying a saucepan intently, opening and closing the fridge door time and again, apparently delighting in the light which sprang up each time she did so. I thought her to be one of nature's originals.

And she was. A gypsy from Granada with exceptionally bandy legs and a voice that could splinter granite. She nodded agreeably at everything I said in complete and total incomprehension, but when I said, 'Okay?', she shrugged and nodded casually, and I wrote down the figure 9 and then 12, meaning the hours she might work. And she, taking my pencil in filthy fingers, laboriously wrote $8\frac{1}{2}$ and $11\frac{1}{2}$ and then made a sign by rubbing her finger and thumb together. I counted out what I felt I could afford in franc notes (Madame Ranchett had advised me), which she accepted with a cackle and a nod. Then she hitched the child on to her hip and wandered down the stairs singing lightly. At the front door she called out in her rasping voice: '*Mañana! Eh!*' And the deal was made.

She stayed with me faithfully and devotedly, for fifteen years, until the time came for me to leave. By then she spoke fairly reasonable French with a disastrous accent, and ran the house with a rod of iron, washed and cleaned and polished, kicked the dogs, and screamed and laughed and worked like a fiend. And grew, deservedly, rich. Her husband, Manolo, came up at weekends, a pleasant man with a hideous scarred face (carved up in a bar room brawl by broken glass) and a fearful squint so that one spoke to the good eye only, the one on the right. He was a good, kind fellow, useful at the olive harvest, changing plugs, pruning the cypress trees every season, and making himself generally useful. She was always called just 'Lady'. Le Pigeonnier functioned smoothly from their arrival onwards.

However, Lady did not cook. And on one occasion when she brought a dish of some wretched famished chicken smothered in rice and saffron as a gift, one was rather relieved. Everything she did was fine – except the cooking.

So, back to square one. An agreement was made: I would be the scullion, that is to say I would wash up, scour saucepans, lay tables, prepare vegetables, empty dustbins and so on, and leave Forwood to do the cooking. In time he moved uneasily, but successfully, far from cauliflower cheese and deep into pilaffs, risottos, soupe au pistou, ratatouille and all manner of other Provençal delights. Pots and pans were bought, knives of astonishing sharpness, mixing-machines, mincing-machines – an entire *batterie de cuisine* formed and I did the washing-up. It took me a very considerable time for the simple reason, as he patiently explained, that cooking was not easy, and that he was what is called a 'messy cook'. That was true. After a simple gigot, flageolets, salad and cheese, it seemed to me that I had to wash up an ironmonger's. I could never understand, really, why? If I made a mild protest it was quietly suggested that I take over. So I shut up . . . and we managed. But I know, I have always known, that I got the worst part of the bargain. And I had to trail off to the market every morning, sharp at seven, winter and summer, to be sure that only the best was bought for this Escoffier of the hillside. I also had to feed the dogs, but as I have said, this was not difficult, and they got better fed now that there was more variety in the green vegetables, not just bits of old cauliflower bunged in with the biscuits. In time, sadly, cheek became prohibitively expensive, and tinned muck came on the market. Easier, cheaper, and somehow the dogs seemed less aggressive to strangers now that they were no longer fed raw flesh. Like bromide in the soldiers' tea, it seemed that tinned food rather took the fizz out of things.

Emigrating to France does not mean that one hurls about the

place looking for a suitable house, buys it, moves in, and lives there happily ever after. There is rather more to it than that. You have to get permission to stay there. At least, you did in my time. France is not just 'any old place', it's not somewhere that you can just dump your belongings and say, 'Here I am.' To begin with, they are not all that anxious to have you. Unless, that is, you intend to return to the land you occupy something from which you have taken, like love, care and attention. I was prepared to offer all that, and more.

But I had chosen to live in a particularly sensitive area, the Alpes Maritimes, bordered with Italy, not far from Switzerland, close to Spain, too close to North Africa. Security was tight. The great hordes of unemployed Arabs from Tunisia and Morocco, the abject poor from Calabria, the drug-pushers, the smugglers of every kind of commodity you can name, would easily swamp the A.M. if not severely curtailed. The ritzy-glitzy crowd who swarmed to Nice and Cannes, played the tables in Monte Carlo, and rented, or bought, hideous villas in the hills were watched carefully, but they never stayed very long and fled at the first signs of inclement weather. Meteorological or political. The people who came to live, that is to live for good, were considered with caution and suspicion.

So, first of all, you had to get your *carte grise*, which permitted you to live in the area for three months. It was a form of identification – your ID card, if you like – and as such, at an accident, a bank or any monetary transaction, always proved extremely useful. At least you knew who you were, so did they, and that in itself was a comfort. In Britain it would be, and it is, 55 considered a breach of privacy. I can't think why. All you have to state is name, birth date, address and, I seem to remember, your mother's name and date of birth. Since *she* was always uncertain and, I feel sure, fibbed about that anyway, it was nothing I took very seriously. But I was pleased to be 'on record'. There was a feeling of security. Don't ask me why.

So, every three months I made the climb up my cliff and through the oakwood at the back of the house to Saint-Cyprien to see the deputy mayor. This had to be done between the hours of five and eight in the evenings. On a fixed date. If you missed it for some reason, you could always try to catch him in the bar he ran in Le Pré. But by that time he really couldn't have signed his name with an X.

So one got to the *mairie* early, sat on a rush-bottomed chair with the other emigrants, the 'legal' Arabs, the Spanish, the Italians. The anteroom was small, whitewashed, red-tiled, spartan, a poster on one wall with a map of France indicating, by a big black dot, the latest advance of rabies, on the other a notice saying when the blood donor caravan would be arriving in the village for the monthly blood donation.

The next stage, after your *carte grise*, literally a bit of grey paper covered with a riot of violet stamps and the deputy's incomprehensible signature, was your *carte de séjour*. This was orange, a proper card, and was a permit to live in, work in and inhabit the Alpes Maritimes. It was a heady moment when that was put in one's wallet. It took for ever to get, and countless journeys, queues and passionate discussions in a vast building in the heart of Nice, where it was always impossible to park a car. However, getting the beastly thing was worth the misery.

Finally – and it took longer than the others, because one's request had to go to Paris, then through officialdom in Nice, and then back to the *mairie* – and finally, one amazing day, you got your blue *carte de résidence*. Not only were you permitted to live in your house, but you had become, apart from voting and joining the army, a French resident. *Taxes compris.* This lasted you for ten years and there were four pages all ready for the stamp ahead. It felt really very good indeed. Because the land had been cared for, because the olives were harvested, the hay cut and sold, because, at first anyway, the sheep grazed, I was classified as an agricultural property and an agricultural proprietor. Which made an enormous difference to my taxes and in the grants made available for the house and· restoration. It felt very secure. Objective gained. With no loss of passport.

Vaguely, at one time, I had thought about taking out French nationality: it was a perplexing idea, but it got pretty swiftly set aside when one realized that it was not impossible that one day, perhaps - perhaps - one could be called upon to fight one's true countrymen. And that, however remote it might have been, was *quite* unthinkable. So one quickly smothered the little spark that had glimmered and concentrated, very hard indeed, on being a good resident.

As the years progressed, the yearly return to England, to see my parents or the family, became slightly depressing. I was starting to feel more and more foreign, I did not quite behave as an Englishman – shaking hands with everyone, calling people 'Madame' or 'Monsieur' (which always caused embarrassment) – generally feeling out of place. Familiar 57 places faded rather. I even forgot the English words for things, and the changes, between 1966 and 1976, for example, became bewildering to me: the behaviour of people; the clothes they wore; the rubbish and filth everywhere; the lack of cafés and brasseries, of reliable trains, mail or general transport to which I had so easily become accustomed – really quite trivial things, I know. But there were other, more alarming things, like the growing envy and spite of the cheap press, hitting at standards which we once had held dear. Perhaps I was out of touch stuck up on my hill in the sun of Provence. Was I spoiled? Had I got it wrong? But I did feel that the quality of life itself was altering, an apathy was growing, with a resentment against anything 'foreign' and therefore unacceptable, cheap, cheating and incomprehensible. I felt, with great reluctance, that we had started to fall back from the race, while on the continent the race was roaring ahead and ready to be won. We seemed to be jellied quite comfortably in aspic. Dunkirk, Vera Lynn, our finest hour and the Blitz! Tourist heaven – but not for today. Surely that was fifty years ago? We were marking time on one spot. Sinking slowly. It was a terribly sad, dusty, uneasy feeling. Driving out to the airport after one of those yearly trips, to catch the early flight home, I drove through the bunting and glory of a full October in the Park: the tumbling leaves, beds of scarlet dahlias, sparkle of the Household Cavalry exercising in the Row, swans on the Serpentine, two youths jogging, their breath drifting like veils in the sharp morning, just-off-frost. Familiar, cherished, but suddenly strange, distant. A complex feeling. Like looking at a sepia

58

photograph of time past, bleached of colour and fine detail, leaving only outline. And then I knew, in one regretful moment, that I now no longer belonged. I was just a visitor in a foreign land.

The 'home stretch' is always the best part of a return. The crunch and scatter of gravel in the lane, rasp and crack of twig, bramble and broom against the bodywork of the car. The spiralling leaves of the big fig, yellow leaflets to announce the end of the season. The overgrown lane winds and dips down past the Meils' farm, she in straw hat, looking up, waving, Emile doffing his beret, leaning on his goat-crook. And then, right ahead, the big stone column built from jagged boulders long since by Fraj, decorated with bits of red glass from a forgotten accident on the corner, the bent chrome letters 'FIAT' crowning its top. His statement.

Winding then slowly up through the still olives, the tended terraces, late sun throwing orange flares from the windows, dogs squealing, barking, racing ahead to the top to greet one. Past the pond, yellowing rushes bending in a late *souffle* of wind, pattering on the water. Henri carrying logs in his arms, waving, his yellow hair spiked and flustered by the breeze, apron flapping, laughing at the dogs. Outside the kitchen, Marie leaning over the balcony rail, vegetable knife in one hand, a head of celery in the other, geranium-red lips bared in a gleaming porcelain smile. Skittering, fighting, snarling from the dogs. Marie laughing, scolding, waving the celery. *'Arrête! Arrête! Tais-toi!'*

'All well, Marie?'

59

'All well, Monsieur: a perfect week. So warm. And London?'

We unpacked luggage. Plastic bags: Harrods, Marks and Spencer, Goode's. Henri bustling up, wiping his hands on his apron, laughing: 'Welcome! Welcome, messieurs.' Lugging suitcases and hand-grips from the boot. Marie calling down, 'Oh là! So much! Did you remember my tea?' Carrying the stuff up the steps on to the balcony, into the kitchen, the smell of simmering lentil soup. 'I remembered your tea. And the Cooper's Oxford. Have they been good? The dogs?' And bending towards the Roman ruin, sitting upright with amber eyes: 'Have you behaved? I have brought you a big yellow ball! From Kensington!' A furiously thumping tail, a scream of jealousy from the other dog who might have been forgotten. Marie crying, 'Poor Daisy! Nothing for Daisy?' Balls were chucked scudding, rumps went bouncing, and belting, into the dusk. Marie, picking up the beech chopping-block left to sweeten in the afternoon sun.

'No one telephoned, not a soul. As the grave here. The mail is in the Long Room.'

'I bought you a present.'

'Tiens...'

'Bendicks Bitter Mints!'

'Mon Dieu! My figure ... my teeth! Oh là!'

Forwood, setting the kettle on the chopping-block, plugging it in, looking for a cup and saucer. We were home.

I have the vegetable knife. Still have the chopping-board. I use them both every day, wondering, sometimes, if all the scratches, cuts and scores, the cross-hatching, the random criss-crossing of long-forgotten knives, this kitchen trigono-metry, is all that is tangible now of a lost lifetime? A worn peeling-knife, a beech chopping-block? Tangible perhaps, yes. Ephemeral, no: there is much more to it all than that.

Titty-Brown Hill was the highest point on my land. A flat-topped, grassy knoll, scarred with clumps of alien corn, it was an easy walk up from the terrace along what was, many, many years before, a cart and cattle track to Saint-Sulpice. On the top it was all absolutely secluded, no one could possibly see a thing; so female guests got into the habit of wandering off up through the sapling oaks and tumbled walls (this area had been rather more neglected than anywhere else) to strip off, happy in their security. The only possible observers of their behaviour would have been the little owl, a chatter of magpies or perhaps an ambling tortoise.

It wasn't very long before the grassy knoll was baptized, and became Titty-Brown Hill. I seemed to have a wish to name parts of the land, or the trees on the land: something to do with knowing, in shorthand language, exactly where one was working, or where work had to be done. For example, if one said, 'I've done all the scything among the five sisters,' it was understood that the two lower terraces beside the path down through the five cypress trees had been cleared. The density of the trees prevented the mowers from raging about, thus causing me to break my back with the scythe but saving the lives of countless lizards, praying mantises, grasshoppers and crickets. Tragically the super-efficient German giants chumbled up the slow-moving insects in vast quantities. A slender stick-insect, even a dashing mantis, simply hadn't a hope in hell of escaping the roaring red machines which whirled them into chaff in a split second.

All the trees which I bought from the nursery in the plain to give my domain instant 'timelessness' were given names so that one would know exactly where one was. 'Charlie' was the tallest, and oldest, and stood hard by the front door, towering over the corrugated pink-tiled roof; 'Rosie' stood like an exclamation mark at the top of the drive; 'Brock' (a nephew) and 'Kimbo' (his wife) shaded the pond. 'Antonia and Eduardo', called after my faithful Spanish staff who had come from England with me to help me get settled down in France, stood beyond the hangar garage and under the kitchen windows. To remind me, if I ever needed reminding, of their loyalty and the sense of loss which they engendered when they, in time, left to go back to Valencia and start up a family, something we had agreed when I left England for abroad. Out of the dozen or so vastly costly trees, only one, called 'Bella', actually slowly died off. Her roots struck a giant rock buried deep under the earth and that settled that.

Thus there were Titty-Brown Hill, Fig Meadow, Long Walk, Pond Lawn, Bamboo Fields, Crescent Lawn, Bonfire Field and so on. They were instantly identifiable if one spoke of them after work in the evenings. 'I've done all round Charlie, and raked up round Brock and Kimbo' meant that the front of the house and the flowerbeds by the terrace had been weeded and the Pond Lawn had been cleared. Simple.

And equally it brought into use the names of much-loved friends or members of the family.

Some of the trees, latterly, were named for the people who had given them as gifts – much more useful and enduring than anything else – and if I was ever asked by some generous guest what to offer as a token of thanks it was always a rose bush, a plant or a sapling tree which proved the most acceptable.

From Titty-Brown you could look out over a giant patchwork of vines, carnations, jasmine, roses, and acres and acres of olive trees. Olive groves, I should perhaps say. Our area was known to produce a particularly excellent fruit, and my land, L'Aire Pigeonnier, was noted for the best olives of all. For years, well, ever since the war, the trees had been neglected badly. The land had flooded from time to time, the trees were saturated and had grown lavishly, producing no fruit. Within about three years (olives fruit only every two years or so) I had once again a good harvest.

At first there were only two of us, Forwood and myself, to do the picking. Crawling about on hands and knees in an anorak and boots, with fingers blue from cold, sodden knees and an aching back, collecting the fallen berries in the frosted grass and wide-spread nets was not at all what I had imagined the olive harvest to be. Fortunately, in time, Monsieur Rémy and Madame Bruna, plus their children, came into the act: they took what they could pick and kept the oil, which provided them with enough virgin-pressing from the mill for a year at least. Our crops were prodigious, and the trip down to the mill in Saint-Sulpice was always one of the splendours of the endeavour.

At dusk, about four o'clock (the harvest started in mid-December and lasted until mid-March), we carted the sacks and buckets down to the village, queued up to get them weighed, took the *fiche* which stated the quantity (to the last gram) we were due, and then tipped the sacks into the great churning mess being crushed and pulped by the giant granite wheel. The scent of the virgin oil, the heavy sweet odour of the brown pulp, with a thread of paraffin wafting from the lamps hung high on the rough stone walls and, above all, the smoke of rough Gitane cigarettes drifting through it, a binding scent for the others, were pungent and immensely comforting. The physical result of hours of back-breaking labour, it was altogether most satisfying.

But quite apart from the vineyards, the roses, carnations, jasmine fields and dense olive groves below Titty-Brown, by far the most exciting, and to some extent worrying, thing was the glorious view over all this land far down to the sea and Africa beyond. Sometimes (fortunately rarely) the great bank of clouds on the distant horizon of the sea would lift for half an hour and the jagged peaks of Corsica, soft pink in the early morning sun, would thrust shimmering high into the pale aching winter sky. I use the words 'worrying' and 'fortunately' here because I had been told often enough by Monsieur Danté that if you could see the mountains on Corsica, then a terrible mistral would shortly arrive. It was time to batten down the hatches, secure the doors and shutters, and huddle in the depths of the huge fireplace under the chimney. Safest place in a really bad mistral or forest fire. Should this occur, then Monsieur Rémy, Danté and Plum-Bum called to each other in concern like chickens, and with a deal of head shaking they would rattle off in the battered truck before the end of the working-day to get their own places ready. You used mostly to see the mountains in the very early morning for some reason. And seldom in summer. When you caught the awesome sight, the mountains were washed by the rising sun glinting on the snows. Corsica has pretty high mountains. Anyway, to see them was not good news, and it always proved to be the case.

Sometimes the mistral would blow for days, and life became extremely miserable: even the dogs crept about wincing, their eyes half closed against the stinging dust, tails curled between their legs, ears flat. The pond turned into a raging sea, waves leapt and bounced, spilling into the rushes, roaring away down the rutted track to the gates in a furious cataract of stones, fish and foaming water. The rain pelted steel arrows, olives writhed and tossed in agony, cypress trees waved, bent and whipped like pheasant plumes. The noise was as savage as a bombardment of rockets. My main anxiety was for the oaks up the rocky hill behind the house: the wind roared and tore among their dense branches with such brutal force that one could only communicate by screaming to each other in short bursts. But, as they'd stood there for many centuries, one prayed they'd hang on a bit longer. And they did, save for a limb or two and bushels of leaves. But they stood stolid and solid. There *were* occasions when the mistral caught us all on the hop, so to speak – then we had to dive for shelter before decapitation from flying roof tiles.

Once we all huddled in the woodshed. Monsieur Danté,
65

Fraj, Plum-Bum and Monsieur Rémy started to scratch at
the wall with a piece of twig. The old whitewash, not yet
restored, flaked away. '*Voyez?* A name?' he said. 'Many
names here, *regardez.*' What I had thought was just a haze of
dust and spiders' webs on the cracked wall were, in fact, tiny
gestures of defiance. Human determination in pencil scrib-
bles; a pattern of anguish from a lost time. Name after name
was criss-crossed on the crumbling plaster. Esthers, Daniels,
Rivkas and Jacobs. All Jewish, all stating, after their names,
the date and the town whence they had come. And their
morale. 'Felix Levant. Avignon. Mai 2 '43. In good heart.
Age 13½.' Across the wall these whispers spread behind the
stacked logs, hanging saws, scythes and coiled hose pipe, the
rakes and *pioches*. Monsieur Rémy pushed his cap to the back
of his head, a habit which he had when concentrating, a
spent match between his gold teeth (in even a moderate
mistral like the present one a cigarette was madness). 'Children. Jewish children. They were collected all over the
region. A brave woman from Paillas. She was a singer before
the war, very noble, proud. She collected the Jewish children,
brought them here, to this house. It was very isolated, the
Germans didn't ever come so far into the valley. When she
had a few together we moved them down to the coast, to La
Napoule . . . some to Théoule . . . Oh! *Malheur!* It was
dangerous! We hid them under the harvest corn, melons,
olives, in carts. From the coast they went by fishing-boat to
the Spanish coast. At night. Not easy, *mon Dieu*, not easy.
We didn't lose *one*! No one gave them away. We stay silent in
Provence.'

Apparently the house itself had been empty for years. Only the land was vaguely tended, and during the early days of 1939 and 1940 a French cavalry regiment had been billeted there with their mounts. After June, and the fall of France, they withdrew and the house mouldered into dust and silence, buried in tall grass, rampant myrtle and ruined olive trees. The village youths, and their girls, were the only people who ever came down the track through the oaks to linger and embrace in the silent rooms.

That was how, and where, he had met Madame Mandelli, staying on a visit from Cremona. Apart from the Jewish children, and these self-exploring adolescents hiding from the eyes of parents and occupiers, Le Pigeonnier was deserted on its tumbled terraces and olives. Monsieur Rémy spat on a finger, drew it through a name. 'Nellie Kaplan. Draguignan. I am well . . .' The rest he wiped away in spittle. 'Long ago. Long ago . . . Perhaps today she has her own children. Eh?'

They all left shortly after, but I told him to leave a part of the wall unpainted when he came to redecorate, as a memorial. He thought I was idiotic. But he thought that of me anyway. But generously. Humour the lunatic. So, anyway, he left a strip untouched. I suppose he was right? It was pretty silly. But they remained. The scribbled defiances and courage.

My father was being evasive. I knew the signs very well. Every time I suggested that we walk down to the little house which I had every intention of securing as a retirement place for him and my mother, if they agreed, he managed to be 67 doing something greatly preoccupying and which he could not leave. 'I'm just getting into the swing of things: I've got the right "mix" for the sky, I always have difficulty with skies, as you know . . . you run along.' Or else he had decided to walk up to the village to buy some cigarettes, or open a beer in the shade, anything as an excuse not to come down through the orchard to the little shuttered house. However, eventually, towards the end of their first visit, I forced the issue and he grudgingly agreed to come with me. 'It's fearfully hot for walking, dear boy. I'm getting on, you know.'

'Nonsense. We'll be in the shade under the trees, and it's all level down to the house. It's a ruin, you realize, but it's full of possibilities and it's mine for £18,000 plus *all* the land. But I *have* to decide by the end of the year.'

'Gun at your head. Wretched business,' said my father.

'No gun at all. Very reasonable. I've had a year to make my decision – it's just over to you really. It's a snip at £18,000, plus a vineyard and three hundred olive trees.'

'I really do prefer a bottle of Worthington, you know. What would we do, your mother and I, with three hundred olive trees? At our age . . . do be reasonable.'

And so we bickered on down the track, ducking under overgrown apple trees, easing through rampant bamboo and tussocky grass, being whipped by heavy blossomed broom. The house, when we reached it, stood like a small stone box.

Facing south, unadorned, a tiled roof, a front door, two floors, a wide dusty track set before it where carts had once turned, with a giant elm of great age shading it from the burning sun. It had almost the same view as that from my house, just slightly tilted to the west, but ahead lay the same valley, the plain, the ridge of the mountains and the silver glitter of the distant sea. I was constantly ravished, my father far less impressed. His pessimism increased as we opened the front door with a big key and trod into the damp-scented dark of the shuttered house.

'It smells like a tunnel! Good God, boy, the place is sodden!'

'It's been empty for years. And I'm told it's surrounded by springs . . . it just needs airing.'

'Needs a charge of dynamite. Rotten with woodworm, I shouldn't wonder. Or damp rot. You can smell it. Wonderful place for mushrooms. You'll make a fortune!'

'Jean-Claude keeps all his work materials here. It can't be *that* damp. He also stores his apples, olives, wine here.'

'That I can smell. Sour stink. Really awful.'

In the narrow hall, tiled floor, staircase ahead, long cracks in the walls, my father stood quite still. 'I think you might open a shutter? Get some light, unless you think they'd fall off?'

They didn't. But the light seemed to compound the scent of decay with the sight of tumbled crates of glass (Jean-Claude was an artist of some kind and made stained-glass windows set in rough concrete), hammers, chisels, buckets and plastic bags from Galeries Lafayette and Casino, filled with hinges, bolts, brackets and yards of rusting chain.

In a corner of one room (there were only two anyway on the ground floor, left and right of the front door), half a dozen wine barrels were ranged along the side of a rough 69 wooden manger. The cracked tile floor was strewn with trodden straw and old, withered apples. I thought it was quite a pleasant smell: fruit, wine, straw. Pa thought otherwise but conceded that he could make a very good little sketch of the still-life before him and started feeling about his pockets for the stub of pencil which he always carried on him, only I got him to come up the stairs and look about. We finally went all over the house. It didn't take three minutes.

Four minute bedrooms, no bathroom, but a staggering view from all the windows. Pa was determinedly unimpressed. 'I do see what you mean. It *has* possibilities. But after securing it for £18,000 you'd have to spend double that on improving it. Damp courses – I bet it's built on a marsh from the stink – bathrooms, new floors and what about drains? And *lavs*? You'll have to instal lavs . . . can't go off into the garden! Not at your mother's age and mine. Good Lord! What a thought!'

'We'd do all that. Of course. It would be a tremendous investment. All this land, peace and quiet . . . off the main road. I really think you'd be very comfortable here. I'd be next door . . .'

Pa walked carefully down the, admittedly, sagging tile staircase holding on anxiously to the thin iron banister. 'You know what your mother would say, don't you? She'd say that she would go mad here in a week. And so she would.'

'Quite mad, darling,' she said at lunch under the vine. 'You are being marvellously dear thinking of Pa and me, but, frankly, at our ages it just wouldn't work. I'd go *quite* mad. What would we do? Stuck up here in the dark? No one to talk to, just sheep. Nowhere to go . . . miles for shopping and your father can't speak French very well.'

'I do, Margaret. I do not badly,' my father protested mildly.

'It's the stuff you learned in that war of yours. It's quite old-fashioned and out of date now . . . No, we simply couldn't manage.'

Pa helped himself to mustard, tapping it briskly on the edge of his plate, concealing impatience. 'Well, I warned you. Your mother is gregarious. Loves people. *Lots* of people. All the time. Amazing really.'

'Oh I do! *I do!* I have to make up for all the years I lost when your father wouldn't let me go back to the theatre. I *need* an audience!'

Pa sighed, reached for his beer. 'I told you . . . it would be impossible.'

'Well, there is nothing to *do* up here,' she said. 'Nothing! I don't know how you and Tote' – Forwood's name in the family – 'can stick it. Perhaps you won't, for long? But for me, just sitting about reading, or sewing or darning. I'd go potty. Anyway, I don't read now . . .'

'Why not? You used to *eat* books.'

'I keep on losing my glasses. Daddy reads to me. Trollope. I ask you . . .'

'Wilkie Collins. You enjoy Wilkie Collins,' said Pa wearily, starting on his *jambon persillé*.

Ma raised her glass and held it up to the sunlight. 'So pretty! Golden. I was bored *witless* by The Woman in White . . . no good pretending. And up here, with bare tiles on the 71 floor and no telephone that really works . . . No, darling, not *us*.'

'I'd rather miss the pub, you know?' said Pa. 'And we have been in Fletching a long time now, got lots of friends there . . . it'd be a wrench to leave. We're very settled in our ways, and that little house down there will always be damp. Built on a marsh, as I said. Interesting idea. But we'll just count this as a splendid holiday, eh?'

My mother usually got her own way, although Pa was pretty stubborn too, so between them I realized that I had lost the chance of the little house and the privacy that the extra acres, adjoining my present land, would give me. But I did see their point. They were nodding at seventy, too late now to alter, and Ma would miss the grandchildren which my brother and sister had provided. So . . . The dream faded, and at the end of the year I had to confront Jean-Claude and regretfully decline the option to buy: he was quite relieved, and said that he really didn't want to sell the last bit of his family's property, after five hundred years, and would use the place as a studio and a store room for his 'work'. He arrived at the house at the hour which we had arranged, on a huge, new, glittering Honda, his long finger-nails painted red, his hair, henna'd as brilliantly as Bruna Mandelli's, falling in long, thin straggles over the shoulders of his expensive leather jacket. Obviously the £75,000 I had paid him for my share of his land had been put to good use. His family, the Marxist wife and a scatter of children, were out of sight somewhere behind the SNCF goods-yard in Nice. A successful man, Jean-Claude. Heaving himself off his bike and attempting to pull it up on to its stand, both he and it fell over.

Forwood muttered something about not slipping a disc and we left him to get to his feet on his own. He was a tall man, angular, with long fingers and longer legs. Petrol poured from the bike, seeping into the dusty path outside the damp house. He struggled for a bit, pulling the bike up, blowing through yellow teeth, brushing his leather jacket, tossing his hair, unsteadily, over his shoulders. There was a pungent smell of pot and petrol; he smiled nonchalantly, and asked me for a front-door key, which he dropped, giggling. I picked it up and he shrugged. '*Gentil*,' he said. '*Félicitations!*' And took it with a mock bow.

In the damp-smelling room with the manger and barrels, he admitted that the place was too damp for anyone to live in; it was, as my father had suggested, built on a marsh. There were many springs in the area, so water would never be our problem even in the intense heat of summer, and that would be very useful if, and when, he would decide to sell up finally, in *years* to come, because he had a secret dream to take his family to a remote place in India and join an ashram, where they would be close to 'life' and 'Krishna'. I asked, unease scratching like a pin in a new shirt, when that might possibly be. He *had* wanted to hold on to the family land? Now he was cheerfully talking about ashrams and India and Krishna and peace and love in a warm climate! He waved a scarlet-tipped hand vaguely, stumbled up the sagging tile staircase and called down, over his shoulder, that he had had the land surveyed in the last few months and that it was quite possible to turn the whole area into an 'up-market *lotissement*'. That is to say, a building-site. They could drain the land, channel the springs and build seven to eight 'high-class villas' on the land my father had so carelessly discarded in favour of his pub in Fletching.

The terrible threat of a *lotissement* and seven or eight 'high-class villas' cast a fearful blight on events for some time to come, but for the moment we were, I thought, safe. Very occasionally the Honda would roar down into the dusty track outside the damp house; there would be a hammering and banging for a time, turquoise sparks flew from some high-powered welding torch, but nothing much else happened. I almost settled down to my usual complacency. Jean-Claude would *never* go to India, they'd never give permission, in this glorious place, for a *lotissement*. And then, one day, some peripheral friends, that is to say people I knew but had never entertained, and by whom I had never been entertained in England, arrived on the coast with their two girls to look 'for somewhere to buy for a holiday home'. The wife, a cheerful, pretty woman, said it would be lovely if we could all meet and perhaps we could give them some advice? About finding a holiday home, I supposed. And I thought of the damp house down the track. Instantly. After all, a pleasant middle-class family with two young girls would be a great deal more attractive than a housing estate of seven or eight villas plus swimming pools. They came up the hill, saw the house, fell instantly in rapturous love with it. Words like 'possibilities', 'peace', 'fantastic views', 'extensions' and so on flew about the place like bats at sundown. They were hooked – I was uncertain, not convinced that I had done quite the right thing. After all, it did mean neighbours, even if it was only for a few weeks in the year when the girls were on holiday from school. And what would Jean-Claude say? He was furious. At first. There was the usual breast-beating about 'family heritage and five hundred years', and then, when I said that the people who wanted the place were a very good family, careful and loving, who would lavish care and taste on the house and restore the olives and the vineyard because money seemed not to be a problem, he became a little more interested and said that he hoped I had not mentioned the price he had offered the property to me for? I assured him that I had not. And I had not. I wasn't such an idiot as that. *I* had the special price for the simple reason that I had been given the year's option on the property before Jean-Claude had come to realize that money could buy him Hondas and henna, or an Indian ashram.

Anyway, after long and contentious telephone calls from London the pleasant family I hardly knew succumbed to Jean-Claude and his lawyers and paid him a sum *far* in excess of the original £18,000 I had been asked for, and possibly in excess of the price I had had to pay for Le Pigeonnier. Jean-Claude really didn't want to sell. He was perfectly happy as things were, but when he heard that the head of the jolly little English family was quite determined to own the damp house and, added to which, would never countenance the word 'No' under any circumstances, he gave in and for this, frankly, bloated amount sold the house on the marsh.

75

Thus I was saved from a huge building-site and got neighbours instead. It worked out pretty well eventually, although I had terrible feelings of guilt and doubt when the drainage diggers started 'next door', and received a shattering blow when they began to prune the three hundred olives.

The hillside beyond my apple trees resembled a John Nash painting or, more explicitly, Passchendaele. It was to look like this for at least two years. And, what was perhaps sadder, was the fact that one morning, on my usual promenade about my land with the dogs, sorting out the jobs to be done in the day, I saw, to my consternation, a vivid crimson slash of paint on a big stone. Bright as a huge gout of blood, the vicious strokes of crimson marked every stone on every terrace from the top road right down the length of my land to the bottom road. Jean-Claude had, quite properly I suppose, marked out the boundary. I found that it was also marked with equal ferocity on the boundary between the de Beauvallons' land on the east. So now we knew where we all belonged.

In time Monsieur Rémy, at my urgent request, erected a long chestnut paling fence down the length of the west boundary, cutting me off from the damp house. It was less intrusive than chain link, and one day, talking with Madame de Beauvallon over sherry in the Long Room, I learned that her son-in-law was about to build a house on her land adjoining mine. Nothing I could do.

They had owned the place, like Jean-Claude, for centuries, it was theirs to do with as they wished. Madame de Beauvallon, because she spoke such good English, was sent to break the unwelcome news. The house, she said, would be very sympathetic, we were above the site so we would never see it, and they would place it so that all the windows faced away from Le Pigeonnier in any case, to take advantage of the view. She was sure we would all get on very well together, and they would plant a great many trees to shelter my privacy. It was all extremely generous and understanding. Only Titty-Brown Hill would suffer. It would be isolated no longer. 'Outside' was closing in.

I always used to prune the big fig tree down by the gates on the morning of Christmas Eve. I can't think at this moment exactly why. Had mournful Monsieur Danté told me, perhaps? He was, when he chose to speak at all, well informed about local agricultural tips. Or perhaps I simply did it out of ignorance? I had never had a fig tree in my life before, until I came to Le Pigeonnier, so it is quite possible that sheer enthusiastic ignorance guided my cutters to the bare branches. The tree was enormous, and hung over the track scratching the paint-work off cars and knocking the postman, on one memorable occasion, off his yellow Mobylette. Christmas time was usually golden and warm. We ate out on the terrace sometimes, always drank our kir royale outside, admired the early marigolds and anemones, rejoiced at the sharp green thrusts of the wild daffodils in the sere grass under the pomegranate, and knew that they were the warning signs alerting us to the fact that the sap was rising and would be surging through the trunks of the big vines on the metal cage above one's head which sheltered the terrace. But that chore, 77 the pruning of the vine down to the last three buds on each branch, had to be done on a certain day at the beginning of February, before the sap had fully risen. It was a brutal business as, armed with monstrously sharp clippers and secateurs, one staggered about dragging ladders and steps, cutting out the prodigal growth of the past year.

The bonfires raged, in a controlled state because of the fire risk, for days. They had to be doused every evening at the end of work with endless cans of water from the well. You can say that it was a remarkable, and exhausting, keep fit class which exercised every muscle you ever had and a good number you didn't know you possessed. It also sweated off pounds in weight. Healthy you would be, exhausted you would be, but proud you would be when the first grey buds blushed pink, burst, and opened tiny green hands to welcome the early spring sunlight. Not an excess length in sight, trim, tied in, perfect; ready to cover the terrace once again and hang its clusters of plump muscat grapes, palest green, translucent as polished jade. They, of course, would bring the vicious *frolon* (hornet) and the lithe, big-eared, yellow-breasted vine rat, which went scampering across the dense growth of leaves and branches, scattering guests in anxious disarray. They were careless creatures and defecated, or urinated, gleefully at will. Hence people's understandable confusion, although, really, few ever received a direct hit. However, that was all to come later, long after Christmas and the cruellest part of the year up on the hill, the vicious January and February. Christmas in France is very unlike the five to six day glut which we seem to endure in England. It only really lasts for a day and a half: Christmas Eve and Christmas Day (even on Christmas Day the bars and bakers are still open). That desperate feeling of having to hoard enough food and drink for almost a week of siege never takes place. Trains run, buses move about. It is merely the celebration of the birth of Christ, and that is celebrated lavishly on Christmas Eve at Midnight Mass.

When they were retired and living in a little flat in the valley, I usually had a tea-party for Marie and Henri, up on the hill, after the fig-pruning. They had no family and no living relatives. Marie would dress up in her best, usually a blue angora or cashmere sweater from Marks and Sparks, thick stockings concealing elastic ones, good white shoes and handbag, and the furious red slash of lipstick. She had her hair 'done': tight, white curls, gently tinted palest lavender. Henri was stuffed, not always comfortably, into a tweed jacket and heavy brogues and sweated. We had Jackson's tea, toast, Gentleman's Relish, Dundee cake, Fox's Ascot biscuits and, if I could make the effort after burning the fig cuttings and laying up the table, cucumber sandwiches. It had to be, at Marie's insistence, a real English tea. There was no point in making the journey up the hill otherwise.

After tea, round the fire, we exchanged presents with little cries of surprise and pleasure, as if we had none of us expected to receive any. The dogs were lavished with love, chewed up the wrapping-paper and string, and everything ended, rather thankfully, with a glass of port. Considered to be correct, heart-warming, rather dashing *and* festive.

Those were the quiet Christmases. Some were busier and, 79

frankly, more fun, especially if the family arrived from England. A bigger adventure, a larger deal for which to cater. But we never had turkey and plum pudding and that stuff. Never saw a cracker or, even worse, a Christmas tree or decorations, which seemed always inappropriate in the sun. Ice clinking in long glasses, melting in the champagne bucket. Bees zooming into the orange and lemon trees heavy with almost sickly scent. Lunch, traditionally, was *boudin blanc*, mashed potato, Brussels sprouts, a giant trifle and a cheese board with fresh fruit. With copious libations of wine. Supper came after Midnight Mass (if one went), with a snack of smoked salmon and hot toast or Brittany oysters before making the journey through the dark, twisting lanes to town and the twelfth-century cathedral.

The bells summonsed us over the hills and little valleys, across the groves and fields. Turning the last corner before climbing up to the town, the cathedral suddenly burst upon the astonished eye lit all over, glowing amber and gold, standing high on the ramparts like an enormous galleon, except galleons don't have towers and belfries; but it *had* a sailing splendour about it. Inside the great doors, the huge stone pillars soared into the shadowy vault of the roof with a faded coat of arms painted on to the planked ceiling. The scent of incense, of hundreds of years of incense, loitered and meandered about, mixing with the fatty smell of melting tallow, as a thousand candles guttered and glittered in the draught, throwing dancing shadows across the rough stone walls, all gold and silver. Honey-light on the limestone pillars, cracked and gouged here and there from a distant, devastating fire which had almost once destroyed the cathedral.

The place was animated by excited chatter, the clatter and scrape of wooden chairs and pews, the patter and clacking of feet, the smothered laughter of sniggering choir boys, the sonorous organ, the flushed expectant faces, the new suits and best coats, the smart hats with little veils, the modest handkerchiefs over modest hair, the dark clothes of the peasants, the sparkier ones of the shop-keepers, the nodding lilies, tuberoses and carnations on the high altar, the soaring Christ, arms outspread, the tall candles, the great oil paintings in elaborate frames, all gilt and curly stucco, glowing from the side walls and the distant little private chapels. There was altogether a jolly, festive air, a feeling of 'coming together', of joining. Some people had journeyed for miles through the hills, and families greeted each other with low calls of pleasure and recognition, bobbing and smiling, the children smothered in nylon net and giant white plastic lace bows, the boys in bow ties and oiled hair. All one's friends were there; discreet little nods and waves across the wooden pews identified us: Madame Bruna and Monsieur Rémy, Madame Pasquini, Florette Ranchett and her disagreeable husband in a sharp grey suit, the Meils flashing silver smiles, the de Beauvallon family in the large family pew, boxed in as befitted the ancient gentry, the bakers, the vet, Dr Santori, the girls from the check-out at Monoprix, the manager of Casino with his sparkling wife a-glitter, rhinestones and faux pearls at wrist and neck, and the very old with sticks, crutches and medals, bent backs and shaking heads. All life was present to celebrate the birth of the Christ child and to worship at his giant crèche, ablaze with fairy lights and worshipping angels, by the great doors.

I enjoyed Christmas Mass very much. The sheer theatricality of it all gave me enormous pleasure. There was absolutely no sense of religion about it as far as I was concerned: the war had put paid to the last embers I might have concealed somewhere deep within. Picking bombing-targets, being responsible for the death of, sometimes, hundreds of people (people just like these at the crèche and before the high altar), blundering into the unspeakable agony of Belsen, watching bulldozers shovel bloodied carnage into open graves, all that and more put paid to religion for me. I went to enjoy the lights, scents and music, in much the same way that I would have attended a village fair: for the excitement, the lights, the fun.

Forwood, from a staunchly Protestant family background, had faint interest in any part of the proceedings (dismissed amusedly as 'popery'), but came along because he could drive and I could not and it would be impolite to the guests who had come for a 'real French Christmas' not to. So they got it, and driving home through the frosted lanes, the stars bright in the southern sky, the hoar heavy in the hollows, embalming grasses and the few remaining leaves on the brambles in white velvet, the crackle of ice on the puddles and the thought of the big iron stove in the Long Room glowing with embers and a big olive log (from the pruning), sighing and flickering across the rough stone walls kept everyone in a joyous mood; to the extent that everyone sang what they could remember of 'Silent Night' in various keys and banished, for a time, its banality. This is how it *should* have sounded. Not as it usually did, droning out as muzak in Monoprix.

Supper at the long walnut table: a giant golden *feuilleté de jambon*, hot from the oven; bowls of salads – tomato, potato, early lettuce, spring onions; cheeses in quantity, if only to prove to the disbelieving British that not *all* French cheeses were Camembert simply because they were round; baguettes crisp, cracked and packed with Normandy butter; wine in brimming goblets. Candles flaring and cries of delight at the arrival of the *bûche de Noël*, a huge 'log' of chocolate, coffee, sugar and sponge-cake, spiked with a robin or two and filled with promises of good luck.

It was all enormous pleasure. The house was bathed in laughter, music and the chink and scraping of plates as Lady and Madame Bruna cleared, set, and chattered and beamed away into the kitchen. By the time we had all finished and the last car had wavered a little uncertainly down the track into the starry, frosty night, one sort of Christmas was finally over, but the ancient house had been alive again with life and happiness. However, it is really true to say, remembering it as now I do, that the best Christmases were really those when the day was just an ordinary day . . . not *quite* ordinary. I remember I always put on a clean shirt, changed my jeans, and there were rather more flowers than I usually allowed myself to buy, anemones in big rough pots, perhaps an azalea from someone, an old Spode footbath planted, ages before, with paper whites and hyacinths. I would bring in the logs at 83 dusk, just as the day faded to night above the mountains, and lights sprang up in the valley and the wind rose. But *ordinary*. That's really what happened every winter evening for a great many years. No one came to feast or for Mass, the dogs slumped snoring before the blazing Godin stove, wide open in vermilion light, Forwood in his chair reading or working at his journal, which he kept faithfully every day. I'd be in my chair scratching away at a drawing for a new book or, more often, correcting and redrafting the work I had done that day in the olive-store office, or studio. Faint on the wind, thin and tinny, the church at Saint-Sulpice clanging the halves and the hour.

It was perhaps pretty dull, although it never occurred to me that it was. I was far too happy to have renounced the cinema, discovered that perhaps I could write a little, which at least paid for some of the bounty with which I was surrounded. It was a very good feeling and even the surprise telephone call, perhaps from some friend in a distant land (I remember Kathleen Tynan once calling from Ontario to send messages of love and bridge the distances) or the family in Sussex, made the day less 'ordinary', but then it is so easy to take security and peace for granted: to accept them, because they have become quite familiar, as just normal. Expected, usual.

I would know, sitting there with my pen, exactly what the remaining hours of that evening would bring: a supper of a sort, a few amber whiskies, shoving the reluctant dogs out for their final pee before bed, and then stoking the stove for the morning, laying up the tea trays, closing the last of the shutters, turning keys, winding up the old wall-clock ...

perfectly normal, routine behaviour stemming from security and contentment.

It never even remotely occurred to me then that all this could be transient, and that as with Bella the cypress tree I had planted with such care and lost years before, this existence was planted above a giant rock buried deep below, and that the 'roots' would one day strike the rock and that the withering would commence. Never once did I really think of that.

I do now.

PENGUIN 60s

MARTIN AMIS · *God's Dice*
HANS CHRISTIAN ANDERSEN · *The Emperor's New Clothes*
MARCUS AURELIUS · *Meditations*
JAMES BALDWIN · *Sonny's Blues*
AMBROSE BIERCE · *An Occurrence at Owl Creek Bridge*
DIRK BOGARDE · *From Le Pigeonnier*
WILLIAM BOYD · *Killing Lizards*
POPPY Z. BRITE · *His Mouth will Taste of Wormwood*
ITALO CALVINO · *Ten Italian Folktales*
ALBERT CAMUS · *Summer*
TRUMAN CAPOTE · *First and Last*
RAYMOND CHANDLER · *Goldfish*
ANTON CHEKHOV · *The Black Monk*
ROALD DAHL · *Lamb to the Slaughter*
ELIZABETH DAVID · *I'll be with You in the Squeezing of a Lemon*
N. J. DAWOOD (TRANS.) · *The Seven Voyages of Sindbad the Sailor*
ISAK DINESEN · *The Dreaming Child*
SIR ARTHUR CONAN DOYLE · *The Man with the Twisted Lip*
DICK FRANCIS · *Racing Classics*
SIGMUND FREUD · *Five Lectures on Psycho-Analysis*
KAHLIL GIBRAN · *Prophet, Madman, Wanderer*
STEPHEN JAY GOULD · *Adam's Navel*
ALASDAIR GRAY · *Five Letters from an Eastern Empire*
GRAHAM GREENE · *Under the Garden*
JAMES HERRIOT · *Seven Yorkshire Tales*
PATRICIA HIGHSMITH · *Little Tales of Misogyny*
M. R. JAMES AND R. L. STEVENSON · *The Haunted Dolls' House*
RUDYARD KIPLING · *Baa Baa, Black Sheep*
PENELOPE LIVELY · *A Long Night at Abu Simbel*
KATHERINE MANSFIELD · *The Escape*

PENGUIN 60s

READ MORE IN PENGUIN

For complete information about books available from Penguin and how to order them, please write to us at the appropriate address below. Please note that for copyright reasons the selection of books varies from country to country.

IN THE UNITED KINGDOM: Please write to *Dept. JC, Penguin Books Ltd, FREEPOST, West Drayton, Middlesex UB7 OBR.*
If you have any difficulty in obtaining a title, please send your order with the correct money, plus ten per cent for postage and packaging, to *PO Box No. 11, West Drayton, Middlesex UB7 OBR.*

IN THE UNITED STATES: Please write to *Consumer Sales, Penguin USA, P.O. Box 999, Dept. 17109, Bergenfield, New Jersey 07621-0120.* VISA and MasterCard holders call 1-800-253-6476 to order all Penguin titles.

IN CANADA: Please write to *Penguin Books Canada Ltd, 10 Alcorn Avenue, Suite 300, Toronto, Ontario M4V 3B2.*

IN AUSTRALIA: Please write to *Penguin Books Australia Ltd, P.O. Box 257, Ringwood, Victoria 3134.*

IN NEW ZEALAND: Please write to *Penguin Books (NZ) Ltd, Private Bag 102902, North Shore Mail Centre, Auckland 10.*

IN INDIA: Please write to *Penguin Books India Pvt Ltd, 706 Eros Apartments, 56 Nehru Place, New Delhi 110 019.*

IN THE NETHERLANDS: Please write to *Penguin Books Netherlands bv, Postbus 3507, NL-1001 AH Amsterdam.*

IN GERMANY: Please write to *Penguin Books Deutschland GmbH, Metzlerstrasse 26, 60594 Frankfurt am Main.*

IN SPAIN: Please write to *Penguin Books S. A., Bravo Murillo 19, 1o B, 28015 Madrid.*

IN ITALY: Please write to *Penguin Italia s.r.l., Via Felice Casati 20, I-20124 Milano.*

IN FRANCE: Please write to *Penguin France S. A., 17 rue Lejeune, F-31000 Toulouse.*

IN JAPAN: Please write to *Penguin Books Japan, Ishikiribashi Building, 2-5-4, Suido, Bunkyo-ku, Tokyo 112.*

IN GREECE: Please write to *Penguin Hellas Ltd, Dimocritou 3, GR-106 71 Athens.*

IN SOUTH AFRICA: Please write to *Longman Penguin Southern Africa (Pty) Ltd, Private Bag X08, Bertsham 2013.*